THE COMPLETE
Plant Based
COOKBOOK

Publications International, Ltd.

Let's get social!

 @Publications_International

 @PublicationsInternational

www.pilbooks.com

TABLE OF CONTENTS

**Cornmeal-Crusted
Cauliflower Steaks**
(page 128)

INTRODUCTION

What is Plant-Based Eating?

Plant-based eating sounds easy. Base your diet on plants, right? Yes, but if you mention plant-based in a room full of people, it will mean something different to everyone.

Opinions vary widely on the definition, and feelings can be heated. People who regularly include meat in their diet may think plant-based is eating more plants along with meat, and perhaps reducing the amount of meat. Those who are already vegetarian may think it means giving up all meat, dairy and eggs completely, while others may say that true plant-based eating means a diet comprised of exclusively organic, local and sustainable plant products, with no dairy, eggs or refined grains, sugar and oils.

So then what is it? The answer is pretty much up to you and how far you want to go. All of the examples above are acceptable, and you may find that you want to transition from eating meat to being vegetarian, and then eliminate all animal products from your diet.

For the purposes of this book, plant-based is defined as always vegetarian and mostly dairy- and egg-free. The important thing, however, is to focus on eating mostly fruit, vegetables and grains and not to get caught up in labels.

If you're just starting out, go easy on yourself and make small positive changes. Adjust your diet incrementally so that you're not overwhelmed with big changes all at once. You want to strike a balance between eating enough plants and making yourself crazy. The first step is to eat more plants and begin to think of meat, eggs and dairy products as garnishes instead of center-of-the plate items.

What Do I Eat Without Meat?

If you're used to thinking of a meal as a protein, a vegetable and a starch, it can be hard to conceptualize a dinner without these traditional elements filling your plate. You can still have that—it just may not look the same as you're used to. For example, Lentils with Pasta on page 150 contains protein (lentils), vegetables (tomatoes, onions) and starch (pasta). It's all mixed up so it may feel like you're only eating one thing but everything is there.

If your usual dinner is cheesy pasta, start with Baked Veggie Mac and Nooch on page 172. The creaminess of cheesy pasta is there thanks to sauce made with nutritional yeast and you've upped your dinner game by adding veggies in the form of a flavorful mix of celery, onion and bell pepper.

If your usual dinner is takeout fried rice or pizza, try Fried Vegetable Rice Noodles on page 154 or Mediterranean Flatbread on page 232 for similar Asian and Italian flavors but with a plantier, healthier spin.

For breakfast, try something easy like Overnight Chia Oat Pudding on page 246. With minimal effort the night before, you'll have a hearty breakfast of grains, fruit and protein ready for you when you need it.

Add More Plants to Your Day

Even on days when you're not up for tons of chopping, you can still easily add vegetables to your day. Roasting is an easy and mostly hands-off way to prepare vegetables for many uses.

First, pick your vegetable(s). Potatoes, sweet potatoes, carrots, cauliflower, broccoli, onions, tomatoes, cabbage, fennel, mushrooms, asparagus, zucchini and winter squash all roast beautifully and deliciously. Next, cut them up into wedges, cubes, sticks or florets, making sure the pieces are approximately the same size.

Then, preheat your oven to 400°F, toss the veggies with olive oil, salt and pepper, and any other seasonings you'd like and spread on a sheet pan. Roast for 20 minutes. Check at this point; some vegetables like carrots may be done. Otherwise, stir the vegetables and add another 10 minutes. Keep checking and stirring until they're as browned and tender as you'd like.

Finally, use them any way you'd like! Here are some ideas to get you started:

- Serve as a side dish or snack with a dip: potatoes with ketchup, sweet potatoes with mustard, carrots with tahini, cauliflower with harissa.

- Use as a topping for flatbread or a filling for sandwiches: onions, garlic, tomatoes, cabbage, fennel, mushrooms, asparagus, butternut squash, zucchini.

- Pick one or two roasted vegetables to add to your favorite pasta or rice dish.

- Chop up cold leftover roasted vegetables and mix with lettuce or mixed greens, chickpeas and your favorite dressing for a veggie-packed salad.

—Tofu

Adding more tofu to your diet can help you move away from meat without feeling like there's a huge hole left behind. Cook up a batch using the method below and toss it with barbecue sauce, hot sauce, teriyaki, pesto, zhug or any other sauce you're craving. Stuff it in a sandwich, layer it in a bowl, or snack on it throughout the day.

Line a sheet pan with foil or parchment paper and lightly brush with oil. Cut the tofu into cubes or rectangles and spread on the pan. Drizzle with soy sauce or sprinkle with salt and toss to coat. Bake at 400°F for 20 minutes or until crispy, turning once. Or use an air fryer if you have one. Cook the tofu at 375°F for 20 minutes or until the tofu is crispy and browned, stirring occasionally.

—Eat Clean

If you're eating a plant-based diet, you may want to incorporate some clean eating strategies as well.

- Eat foods in their natural state (or as close as possible).

- Avoid processed foods, refined sugars (white sugar) and refined grains (white flour).

- Plan your meals and go shopping with a list. This way you'll be less tempted by unhealthy foods.

- Go through your pantry and get rid of anything old, stale or processed. You'll start fresh and know what you have.

- Stock up on canned beans, tomatoes, water-packed fruit, brown rice, whole wheat pasta, olive oil and frozen veggies. A quick and healthy plant-based meal will be at the ready and you'll feel less tempted to make unhealthy choices.

Colorful Coleslaw

¼ **head green cabbage, shredded or thinly sliced**

¼ **head red cabbage, shredded or thinly sliced**

1 **small yellow or orange bell pepper, thinly sliced**

1 **small jicama, peeled and julienned**

¼ **cup thinly sliced green onions**

2 **tablespoons chopped fresh cilantro**

Dressing

¼ **cup vegetable oil**

¼ **cup fresh lime juice**

1 **teaspoon salt**

⅛ **teaspoon black pepper**

1. Combine green cabbage, red cabbage, bell pepper, jicama, green onions and cilantro in large bowl.

2. Whisk oil, lime juice, salt and black pepper in small bowl until well blended. Pour over vegetables; toss to coat. Cover; refrigerate 2 to 6 hours for flavors to blend.

———— **Makes 4 to 6 servings**

Note: This coleslaw makes a great topping for tacos and sandwiches.

Superfood Kale Salad

Carrots

8 carrots, trimmed

2 tablespoons olive oil

2 tablespoons maple syrup

½ teaspoon salt

⅛ teaspoon black pepper

Dash ground red pepper

Dressing

¼ cup olive oil

3 tablespoons lemon juice

2 tablespoons maple syrup

¾ teaspoon grated lemon peel

½ teaspoon salt

⅛ teaspoon black pepper

Salad

4 cups chopped kale

2 cups chopped mixed greens

1 cup dried cranberries

1 cup slivered almonds, toasted*

½ cup shredded Parmesan cheese (optional)

To toast almonds, cook in medium skillet over medium heat 3 to 4 minutes or until lightly browned and fragrant, stirring frequently.

1. Preheat oven to 400°F. Line baking sheet with parchment paper.

2. Place carrots on prepared baking sheet. Whisk 2 tablespoons oil, 2 tablespoons maple syrup, ½ teaspoon salt, ⅛ teaspoon black pepper and red pepper in small bowl until well blended. Brush some of oil mixture over carrots. Roast 30 minutes or until carrots are tender, brushing with oil mixture and shaking baking sheet every 10 minutes. Cut carrots crosswise into ¼-inch slices when cool enough to handle.

3. Meanwhile for dressing, whisk ¼ cup oil, lemon juice, 2 tablespoons maple syrup, lemon peel, ½ teaspoon salt and ⅛ teaspoon black pepper in small bowl until well blended.

4. Combine kale, greens, cranberries and almonds in large bowl. Add carrots. Pour vinaigrette over salad; toss to coat. Top with cheese, if desired.

—— **Makes 4 servings**

House Salad

1 cup croutons, store-bought or homemade (recipe follows)

Dressing

½ cup regular or vegan mayonnaise

¼ cup white wine vinegar

¼ cup grated Parmesan cheese or nutritional yeast

1 tablespoon olive oil

1 tablespoon lemon juice

1 tablespoon corn syrup

1 clove garlic, minced

¾ teaspoon Italian seasoning

½ teaspoon salt

½ teaspoon black pepper

Salad

1 package (10 ounces) Italian salad blend

2 plum tomatoes, thinly sliced

½ cup thinly sliced red or green bell pepper

½ cup thinly sliced red onion

¼ cup sliced black olives

Pepperoncini peppers (optional)

1. Prepare croutons, if desired.

2. For dressing, whisk mayonnaise, vinegar, cheese, oil, lemon juice, corn syrup, garlic, Italian seasoning, salt and black pepper in medium bowl until well blended.

3. For salad, place salad blend in large bowl; top with tomatoes, croutons, bell pepper, onion, olives and pepperoncini, if desired. Add dressing; toss to coat.

—— Makes 4 servings

Homemade Croutons: Preheat oven to 350°F. Cut any kind of bread into cubes (hearty bread like whole wheat, Tuscan or sourdough works best, but sandwich bread works, too). Spread the bread on a sheet pan and drizzle with olive oil. Toss to coat. The bread should be evenly coated; add more oil if needed and toss again. Season with salt and pepper and dried herbs like oregano, thyme or rosemary. Bake 10 to 15 minutes or until golden brown, stirring once or twice. Cool completely before using.

Pineapple Ginger Slaw with Quinoa

Salad

- ½ cup uncooked tricolor quinoa
- 1 cup water
- ¾ teaspoon salt, divided
- 4 cups shredded red cabbage
- 1 poblano pepper, thinly sliced
- ½ cup chopped red onion
- ½ cup chopped fresh mint
- 1 can (8 ounces) pineapple tidbits, drained

Dressing

- 3 tablespoons sugar
- 3 tablespoons lime juice
- 2 tablespoons canola oil
- 2 teaspoons grated fresh ginger
- Black pepper (optional)

1. Rinse quinoa under cold water in fine-mesh strainer. Bring 1 cup water, quinoa and ¼ teaspoon salt to a boil in small saucepan. Reduce heat to low; cover and simmer 10 to 15 minutes or until quinoa is tender and water is absorbed. Place quinoa in fine-mesh strainer; rinse under cold water to cool.

2. Combine cabbage, poblano pepper, onion and mint in large bowl; stir in quinoa and pineapple.

3. For dressing, whisk sugar, lime juice, oil, ginger and remaining ½ teaspoon salt in small bowl until well blended. Pour over salad; mix well. Season with black pepper, if desired.

—— Makes 6 servings

Crunchy Jicama, Radish and Melon Salad

Salad

- 3 cups julienned jicama
- 3 cups cubed watermelon
- 2 cups cubed cantaloupe
- 1 cup sliced radishes

Dressing

- 3 tablespoons chopped fresh cilantro
- 2 tablespoons olive oil
- 2 tablespoons lime juice
- 1 tablespoon orange juice
- 1 tablespoon cider vinegar
- 1 tablespoon honey
- ½ teaspoon salt

1. Combine jicama, watermelon, cantaloupe and radishes in large bowl.

2. For dressing, whisk cilantro, oil, lime juice, orange juice, vinegar, honey and salt in small bowl until smooth and well blended. Add to salad; gently toss to coat evenly. Serve immediately.

—— Makes 8 servings

Quinoa and Cauliflower Taco Salad

¾ cup uncooked quinoa

1½ cups water

4 cloves garlic, minced, divided

1 tablespoon chili powder

1¾ teaspoons salt, divided

1¼ teaspoons ground cumin, divided

½ teaspoon dried oregano

¼ cup plus 2 teaspoons olive oil, divided

4 cups coarsely chopped cauliflower

½ cup raw pepitas

Juice of 1 lime

Salt and black pepper

4 to 6 cups shredded iceberg lettuce

2 large tomatoes, diced

2 avocados, diced

Cheddar-style vegan cheese alternative shreds (optional)

Crispy tortilla strips or crumbled tortilla chips

1. Rinse quinoa in fine-mesh strainer under cold water. Place in medium saucepan. Add 1½ cups water, 3 cloves garlic, chili powder, 1 teaspoon salt, 1 teaspoon cumin and oregano. Bring to a boil over medium-high heat. Reduce heat to low; cover and simmer 15 minutes or until quinoa is tender and water is absorbed.

2. Meanwhile, heat 1 teaspoon oil in large nonstick skillet over medium-high heat. Add cauliflower and ½ teaspoon salt; cook and stir 10 minutes or until tender and browned. Add quinoa to cauliflower; cook and stir until well blended.

3. Heat 1 teaspoon oil in small skillet over medium heat. Add pepitas; cook and stir 3 to 5 minutes or until pepitas begin to pop and are lightly browned. Season with remaining ¼ teaspoon salt.

4. For dressing, whisk remaining ¼ cup oil, ¼ teaspoon cumin and lime juice in medium bowl until well blended. Season with salt and pepper.

5. Arrange lettuce on large serving platter. Top with quinoa mixture, tomatoes, avocados, cheese alternative, if desired, pepitas and tortilla strips. Serve with dressing.

—— Makes 8 servings

Roasted Brussels Sprouts Salad

Brussels Sprouts

- **1 pound brussels sprouts, trimmed and halved**
- **2 tablespoons olive oil**
- **½ teaspoon salt**

Salad

- **2 cups coarsely chopped baby kale**
- **2 cups coarsely chopped romaine lettuce**
- **1½ cups candied pecans**
- **1 cup halved red grapes**
- **1 cup diced cucumbers**
- **½ cup dried cranberries**
- **½ cup fresh blueberries**
- **½ cup chopped red onion**
- **¼ cup toasted pepitas**
- **1 container (4 ounces) crumbled goat cheese (optional)**

Dressing

- **½ cup olive oil**
- **6 tablespoons balsamic vinegar**
- **6 tablespoons strawberry jam**
- **2 teaspoons Dijon mustard**
- **1 teaspoon salt**

1. For brussels sprouts, preheat oven to 400°F. Spray large baking sheet with nonstick cooking spray.

2. Combine brussels sprouts, 2 tablespoons oil and ½ teaspoon salt in medium bowl; toss to coat. Arrange brussels sprouts in single layer, cut sides down, on prepared baking sheet. Roast 20 minutes or until tender and browned, stirring once halfway through roasting. Cool completely on baking sheet.

3. For salad, combine kale, lettuce, pecans, grapes, cucumbers, cranberries, blueberries, onion and pepitas in large bowl. Top with brussels sprouts and cheese, if desired.

4. For dressing, whisk ½ cup oil, vinegar, jam, mustard and 1 teaspoon salt in small bowl until well blended. Pour dressing over salad; toss gently to coat.

—— **Makes 6 servings (about 8 cups)**

Note: Glazed or candied pecans may be found in the produce section of the supermarket with other salad toppings, or they may be found in the snack aisle.

Pepita Lime Cabbage Slaw

½ **red onion, thinly sliced**

3 **tablespoons apple cider vinegar**

1 **teaspoon sugar**

2½ **teaspoons salt, divided**

½ **teaspoon ground cumin**

¼ **teaspoon onion powder**

⅛ **teaspoon ground coriander**

⅛ **teaspoon celery seed**

1 **tablespoon plus 2 teaspoons olive oil**

½ **cup raw pepitas**

⅛ **teaspoon black pepper**

4 **cups thinly sliced green cabbage (about ⅛ head)**

4 **cups thinly sliced red cabbage (about ½ small head)**

3 **tablespoons chopped fresh cilantro**

2 **tablespoons lime juice**

1. Place onion in large bowl. Add vinegar, sugar and 1 teaspoon salt; mix well. Let stand at least 20 minutes.

2. Combine cumin, onion powder, coriander, celery seed and 1 teaspoon salt in small bowl.

3. Meanwhile, heat 2 teaspoons oil in small skillet over medium heat. Add pepitas; cook and stir 3 to 5 minutes or until pepitas are starting to brown and pop. Season with remaining ½ teaspoon salt and pepper. Remove to plate; cool completely.

4. Add green cabbage, red cabbage and cilantro to onion in large bowl. Drizzle with remaining 1 tablespoon oil and lime juice and sprinkle with seasoning mix. Mix thoroughly with hands, squeezing to blend everything evenly. Sprinkle with pepitas; toss gently to blend.

—— **Makes 6 to 8 servings**

Hot and Spicy Fruit Salad

Dressing

- ⅓ cup orange juice
- 3 tablespoons lime juice
- 1 tablespoon honey
- 2 jalapeño peppers, seeded and minced
- 3 tablespoons minced fresh mint, basil or cilantro

Salad

- ½ small honeydew melon, cut into cubes
- 1 ripe large papaya, peeled, seeded, cubed
- 1 pint fresh strawberries, stemmed, halved
- 1 can (8 ounces) pineapple chunks, drained

1. For dressing, whisk orange juice, lime juice and honey in medium bowl until blended. Stir in jalapeños and mint.

2. Combine melon, papaya, strawberries and pineapple in large bowl. Pour dressing over fruit; toss gently until well blended.

3. Serve immediately or cover and refrigerate up to 3 hours.

—— Makes 6 servings

Crunchy Mandarin Orange Salad

Dressing

⅓ cup olive oil

2 tablespoons cider vinegar

2 teaspoons honey

2 teaspoons dried tarragon

½ teaspoon dry mustard

¼ teaspoon salt

⅛ teaspoon black pepper

1 can (11 ounces) mandarin oranges, drained and 1 tablespoon juice reserved

Salad

4 cups chopped romaine lettuce

1 package (3 ounces) ramen noodles, any flavor, crumbled*

½ cup toasted pecans, coarsely chopped**

¼ cup chopped red onion

Discard seasoning packet.

**To toast pecans, cook in medium skillet over medium heat 3 to 4 minutes or until lightly browned and fragrant, stirring frequently.*

1. For dressing, whisk oil, vinegar, honey, tarragon, mustard, salt, pepper and reserved orange juice in large bowl.

2. Add lettuce, oranges, crumbled noodles, pecans and onion to dressing; toss to combine.

—— Makes 4 servings

Edamame Peanut Slaw

Salad

4 cups thinly sliced green cabbage (about ⅛ head)

3 cups thinly sliced red cabbage (about ½ small head)

1 red bell pepper, thinly sliced

1 cup thawed frozen shelled edamame

3 green onions, thinly sliced

1 carrot, shredded or julienned

Dressing

Juice of 1 lime

2 tablespoons unseasoned rice vinegar

1 tablespoon toasted sesame oil

2 teaspoons salt

1 teaspoon sugar

1 teaspoon minced fresh ginger

1 cup roasted peanuts

1. Combine green cabbage, red cabbage, bell pepper, edamame, green onions and carrot in large bowl.

2. For dressing, whisk lime juice, vinegar, oil, salt, sugar and ginger in small bowl until salt and sugar are dissolved. Pour dressing over salad; mix well. Stir in peanuts just before serving.

—— **Makes 6 to 8 servings**

Note: This slaw can be made a day ahead and will even be good for several days. Store in a covered bowl or container and adjust the salt, lime juice and vinegar before serving. For crunchy peanuts, stir them in just before serving. They will also be fine if you stir them in early and let them sit; their texture will be more crisp-tender than crisp, similar to the edamame.

Chickpea Pasta Salad

Salad

4 ounces uncooked spinach rotini or fusilli pasta

1 can (about 15 ounces) chickpeas, rinsed and drained

½ cup chopped red bell pepper

⅓ cup chopped celery

⅓ cup finely chopped carrot

2 green onions, chopped

Dressing

3 tablespoons balsamic vinegar

2 tablespoons regular or vegan mayonnaise

2 teaspoons whole grain mustard

½ teaspoon black pepper

¼ teaspoon Italian seasoning

Salt (optional)

Leaf lettuce

1. Cook pasta in large saucepan of salted boiling water according to package directions for al dente. Rinse under cold water until cool; drain well.

2. Combine pasta, chickpeas, bell pepper, celery, carrot and green onions in medium bowl.

3. For dressing, whisk vinegar, mayonnaise, mustard, black pepper and Italian seasoning in small bowl until blended. Pour over salad; toss to coat. Season with salt, if desired. Cover and refrigerate up to 8 hours.

4. Arrange lettuce on serving plates; top with salad.

—— **Makes 4 to 6 servings**

Lime-Ginger Coleslaw

Salad

2 cups shredded green cabbage

1½ cups julienned or shredded carrots

1 cup shredded red cabbage

¼ cup finely chopped green onions

Dressing

3 tablespoons lime juice

2 tablespoons sugar or agave nectar

2 tablespoons chopped fresh cilantro

2 teaspoons vegetable or canola oil

1½ teaspoons grated fresh ginger

½ teaspoon salt

⅛ teaspoon red pepper flakes or black pepper

1. Combine green cabbage, carrots, red cabbage and green onions in large bowl; toss well.

2. For dressing, whisk lime juice, sugar, cilantro, oil, ginger, salt and red pepper flakes in small bowl. Pour over salad; let stand at least 10 minutes before serving.

—— **Makes 4 servings**

Meal Idea: Serve with Tofu Satay with Peanut Sauce (page 196) and hot cooked white rice.

Kale Salad with Cherries and Avocados

¼ cup plus 1 teaspoon olive oil, divided

3 tablespoons uncooked quinoa

¾ teaspoon salt, divided

3 tablespoons balsamic vinegar

1 tablespoon red wine vinegar

1 tablespoon maple syrup

2 teaspoons Dijon mustard

¼ teaspoon dried oregano

⅛ teaspoon black pepper

1 large bunch kale (about 1 pound)

1 package (5 ounces) dried cherries

2 avocados, diced

½ cup smoked almonds, chopped

1. Heat 1 teaspoon oil in small saucepan over medium-high heat. Add quinoa; cook and stir 3 to 5 minutes or until quinoa is golden brown and popped. Season with ¼ teaspoon salt. Remove to plate; cool completely.

2. Combine balsamic vinegar, red wine vinegar, maple syrup, mustard, oregano, pepper and remaining ½ teaspoon salt in medium bowl. Whisk in remaining ¼ cup oil until well blended.

3. Place kale in large bowl. Pour dressing over kale; massage dressing into leaves until well blended and kale is slightly softened. Add popped quinoa; stir until well blended. Add cherries, avocados and almonds; toss until blended.

—— **Makes 6 to 8 servings**

Southwest Tossed Salad

Tortilla Strips

2 (6-inch) flour tortillas

1 teaspoon vegetable oil

Dash paprika

Dressing

¼ cup orange juice

1 tablespoon white wine vinegar

1 tablespoon olive oil

4 cloves garlic, minced

¼ teaspoon ground cumin

¼ teaspoon black pepper

Salad

3 cups torn romaine leaves

1 cup torn Boston lettuce leaves

1 cup julienned jicama

2 medium oranges, cut into segments

1 medium tomato, cut into wedges

¼ cup thinly sliced red onion

1. For tortilla strips, preheat oven to 375°F. Cut tortillas into halves; cut halves into ¼-inch-wide strips. Arrange tortilla strips on baking sheet. Drizzle with vegetable oil; toss to coat. Sprinkle with paprika. Bake about 10 minutes or until browned, stirring occasionally. Let cool to room temperature.

2. For dressing, combine orange juice, vinegar, olive oil, garlic, cumin and pepper in small jar with tight-fitting lid; shake well. Refrigerate until ready to use.

3. Combine lettuces, jicama, oranges, tomato and onion in large bowl. Shake dressing; pour over salad and toss gently to coat. Sprinkle with tortilla strips.

—— **Makes 4 servings**

SOUPS & STEWS

Garden Vegetable Soup

1 tablespoon olive oil

1 medium onion, chopped

1 carrot, chopped

1 stalk celery, chopped

1 medium zucchini, diced

1 medium yellow squash, diced

1 red bell pepper, diced

2 tablespoons tomato paste

2 cloves garlic, minced

2 teaspoons salt

1 teaspoon Italian seasoning

½ teaspoon black pepper

8 cups vegetable broth

1 can (28 ounces) whole tomatoes, chopped, juice reserved

½ cup uncooked pearl barley

1 cup cut green beans (1-inch pieces)

½ cup corn

¼ cup slivered fresh basil

1 tablespoon lemon juice

1. Heat oil in large saucepan or Dutch oven over medium-high heat. Add onion, carrot and celery; cook and stir 8 minutes or until vegetables are softened. Add zucchini, yellow squash and bell pepper; cook and stir 5 minutes or until softened. Stir in tomato paste, garlic, salt, Italian seasoning and black pepper; cook 1 minute. Stir in broth and tomatoes with juice; bring to a boil. Stir in barley.

2. Reduce heat to low; cook 30 minutes. Stir in green beans and corn; cook about 15 minutes or until barley is tender and green beans are crisp-tender. Stir in basil and lemon juice.

—— Makes 8 to 10 servings

Fasolada (Greek White Bean Soup)

4 tablespoons olive oil, divided

1 large onion, diced

3 stalks celery, diced

3 carrots, diced

4 cloves garlic, minced

¼ cup tomato paste

1 teaspoon salt

1 teaspoon dried oregano

½ teaspoon ground cumin

¼ teaspoon black pepper

1 bay leaf

4 cups vegetable broth

3 cans (about 15 ounces each) cannellini beans, rinsed and drained

2 tablespoons lemon juice

¼ cup minced fresh parsley

1. Heat 2 tablespoons oil in large saucepan over medium-high heat. Add onion, celery and carrots; cook and stir 8 to 10 minutes or until vegetables are softened. Stir in garlic; cook and stir 30 seconds. Stir in tomato paste, salt, oregano, cumin, pepper and bay leaf; cook and stir 30 seconds.

2. Stir in broth; bring to a boil. Stir in beans; return to a boil. Reduce heat to medium-low; simmer 30 minutes. Stir in remaining 2 tablespoons oil and lemon juice. Remove and discard bay leaf. Sprinkle with parsley just before serving.

====== **Makes 4 to 6 servings**

West African Peanut Soup

2 tablespoons vegetable oil

1 large onion, chopped

½ cup chopped roasted peanuts

1½ tablespoons minced fresh ginger

4 cloves garlic, minced (about 1 tablespoon)

1 teaspoon salt

4 cups vegetable broth

2 sweet potatoes, peeled and cut into ½-inch cubes

1 can (28 ounces) whole tomatoes, drained and coarsely chopped

¼ teaspoon ground red pepper

1 bunch Swiss chard or kale, stemmed and shredded

⅓ cup unsweetened peanut butter (creamy or chunky)

1. Heat oil in large saucepan over medium-high heat. Add onion; cook and stir 5 minutes or until softened. Add peanuts, ginger, garlic and salt; cook and stir 1 minute. Stir in broth, sweet potatoes, tomatoes and red pepper; bring to a boil. Reduce heat to medium; simmer 10 minutes.

2. Stir in chard and peanut butter; cook over medium-low heat 10 minutes or until vegetables are tender and soup is creamy.

—— **Makes 6 to 8 servings**

Mexican Tortilla Soup

6 (6-inch) corn tortillas, preferably day-old

2 large very ripe tomatoes (about 1 pound), peeled, seeded and cut into chunks

⅔ cup coarsely chopped white onion

1 clove garlic

Vegetable oil

7 cups vegetable broth

4 sprigs fresh cilantro

3 sprigs fresh mint (optional)

½ to 1 teaspoon salt

4 or 5 dried pasilla chiles

7 to 8 ounces firm or silken tofu, cut into ½-inch cubes

¼ cup coarsely chopped fresh cilantro

1. Stack tortillas; cut stack into ½-inch-wide strips. Let tortilla strips stand, uncovered, on wire rack 1 to 2 hours to dry slightly.

2. Combine tomatoes, onion and garlic in blender or food processor; blend until smooth. Heat 3 tablespoons oil in large saucepan over medium heat until hot. Add tomato mixture; cook 10 minutes, stirring frequently. Add broth and cilantro sprigs; bring to a boil over high heat. Reduce heat to low; simmer, uncovered, 20 minutes. Add mint sprigs, if desired, and salt; simmer 10 minutes. Remove and discard cilantro and mint sprigs. Keep soup warm.

3. Heat ½ inch of oil in large deep skillet over medium-high heat to 375°F; adjust heat to maintain temperature. Fry half of tortilla strips in single layer 1 minute or until crisp, turning occasionally. Remove with slotted spoon; drain on paper towel-lined plate. Repeat with remaining tortilla chips.

4. Fry chiles in same oil about 30 seconds or until puffed and crisp, turning occasionally. *Do not burn chiles.* Drain on paper towel-lined plate. Cool slightly; crumble into coarse pieces.

5. Ladle soup into bowls; serve with chiles, tortilla strips, tofu and chopped cilantro.

—— **Makes 4 to 6 servings**

Sweet Potato and Black Bean Chipotle Chili

1 tablespoon vegetable oil

1 large onion, chopped

2 cloves garlic, minced

2 tablespoons tomato paste

2 tablespoons chili powder

1 teaspoon ground chipotle pepper

1 teaspoon ground cumin

1 teaspoon salt

½ cup water

1 large sweet potato, peeled and cut into ½-inch pieces

1 can (28 ounces) black beans, rinsed and drained

1 can (28 ounces) crushed tomatoes

Sliced green onions and corn chips

1. Heat oil in large saucepan over medium-high heat. Add onion; cook and stir 8 minutes or until softened and lightly browned. Add garlic, tomato paste, chili powder, chipotle pepper, cumin and salt; cook and stir 1 minute. Add water, stirring to scrape up browned bits from bottom of saucepan.

2. Add sweet potato, beans and tomatoes; bring to a boil. Reduce heat to low; simmer 30 to 40 minutes or until sweet potato is tender.

3. Ladle into bowls. Serve with green onions and corn chips.

—— Makes 8 to 10 servings

Quick Bean, Tomato and Spinach Soup

1 tablespoon plus
   2 teaspoons olive
   oil, divided

1 onion, chopped

2 cans (about 14 ounces
   each) diced tomatoes

1 can (about 14 ounces)
   vegetable broth

2 teaspoons sugar

2 teaspoons dried basil

1 teaspoon salt

¾ teaspoon soy sauce

1 can (about 15 ounces)
   small white beans,
   rinsed and drained

1 package (5 ounces) baby
   spinach

1. Heat 1 tablespoon oil in Dutch oven or large saucepan over medium-high heat. Add onion; cook and stir 5 minutes or until softened. Add tomatoes, broth, sugar, basil, salt and soy sauce; bring to a boil. Reduce heat to low. Simmer, uncovered, 10 minutes.

2. Stir in beans and spinach; cook 5 minutes or until spinach is tender.

3. Remove from heat; stir in remaining 2 teaspoons oil just before serving.

—— **Makes 4 servings**

Middle Eastern Eggplant Stew

¼ cup olive oil

3 cups sliced zucchini

2 cups cubed peeled eggplant

2 cups sliced quartered peeled sweet potatoes

1 can (28 ounces) crushed tomatoes in purée

1 cup drained canned chickpeas

1½ teaspoons ground cinnamon

1 teaspoon grated orange peel

¾ teaspoon ground cumin

½ teaspoon salt

½ teaspoon paprika

¼ to ½ teaspoon ground red pepper

⅛ teaspoon ground cardamom

Hot cooked whole wheat couscous or brown rice (optional)

1. Heat oil in Dutch oven or large saucepan over medium heat. Add zucchini, eggplant and sweet potatoes; cook and stir 8 to 10 minutes or until vegetables are slightly softened. Stir in tomatoes, chickpeas, cinnamon, orange peel, cumin, salt, paprika, ground red pepper and cardamom; bring to a boil over high heat.

2. Reduce heat to low; cover and simmer 30 minutes or until vegetables are tender. If sauce becomes too thick, stir in water to reach desired consistency. Serve over couscous, if desired.

—— **Makes 6 servings**

Hearty White Bean and Kale Soup

1 tablespoon olive oil

1 medium onion, chopped

3 carrots, chopped

3 stalks celery, chopped

2 cloves garlic, minced

½ teaspoon salt

¼ teaspoon black pepper

5 cups vegetable broth

2 cans (about 15 ounces each) cannellini beans, rinsed and drained

2 russet potatoes, peeled and cut into ½-inch cubes

1 can (about 14 ounces) diced tomatoes

6 cups chopped fresh kale

1. Heat oil in large saucepan over medium-high heat. Add onion, carrots and celery; cook and stir 10 minutes or until softened. Stir in garlic, salt and pepper; cook and stir 30 seconds. Stir in broth, beans, potatoes and tomatoes. Bring to a boil. Reduce heat to medium-low; simmer 30 minutes or until potatoes are fork-tender.

2. Stir in kale; cook 10 to 15 minutes or until kale is tender.

—— **Makes 6 servings**

Note: This recipe can be made in a slow cooker. Combine all ingredients except kale in a slow cooker. Cover and cook on LOW 7 hours. Turn slow cooker to HIGH. Stir in kale; cook 1 to 2 hours or until vegetables are tender.

Pasta e Fagioli

2 tablespoons olive oil

1 cup chopped onion

3 cloves garlic, minced

2 cans (about 14 ounces each) Italian-style stewed tomatoes, undrained

3 cups vegetable broth

1 can (about 15 ounces) cannellini beans or Great Northern beans, undrained

¼ cup chopped fresh parsley

1 teaspoon dried basil

½ teaspoon salt

¼ teaspoon black pepper

4 ounces uncooked small shell pasta

1. Heat oil in Dutch oven or large saucepan over medium heat. Add onion and garlic; cook and stir 5 minutes or until onion is tender.

2. Add tomatoes, broth, beans with liquid, parsley, basil, salt and pepper to Dutch oven; bring to a boil over high heat, stirring occasionally. Reduce heat to low. Cover and simmer 10 minutes.

3. Add pasta to Dutch oven. Cover; simmer 10 minutes or just until pasta is tender. Serve immediately.

—— **Makes 4 servings**

Vegetable and Barley Chili

1⅔ cups water

1½ teaspoons salt, divided

⅔ cup quick-cooking pearl
     barley

1 tablespoon olive or
   vegetable oil

1 large red or sweet onion,
   finely chopped

2 cloves garlic, minced

4 medium tomatoes,
   coarsely chopped*

4 cups chopped mixed
   vegetables such as
   zucchini, green beans,
   cauliflower and/or
   broccoli

2 cans (about 14 ounces
   each) tomato sauce

2 tablespoons chili powder

2 teaspoons ground cumin

1 teaspoon dried oregano

¼ teaspoon black pepper

¼ teaspoon red pepper
   flakes

*Or use 1 can (28 ounces) diced
tomatoes.

1. Bring water and ½ teaspoon salt to a boil in small saucepan. Stir in barley. Reduce heat to medium-low; cover and simmer 10 minutes or until tender. Let stand, covered, 5 minutes. Drain any remaining liquid.

2. Meanwhile, heat oil in large skillet over medium-high heat. Add onion and garlic; cook and stir 5 minutes or until tender. Add tomatoes. Reduce heat to medium; cook and stir 2 minutes. Stir in vegetables; cook and stir 5 minutes or until beginning to soften.

3. Add barley, tomato sauce, chili powder, remaining 1 teaspoon salt, cumin, oregano, black pepper and red pepper flakes. Cover and simmer 15 to 20 minutes or until vegetables are tender and flavors have blended.

—— **Makes 4 servings**

Rustic Vegetable Soup

2 russet potatoes, peeled and cut into ½-inch pieces

1 bag (10 ounces) frozen mixed vegetables, thawed

1 bag (10 ounces) frozen cut green beans, thawed

1 medium green bell pepper, chopped

1 jar (16 ounces) picante sauce

1 can (about 14 ounces) vegetable broth

½ teaspoon salt

½ teaspoon sugar

¼ cup finely chopped fresh parsley

Slow Cooker Directions

1. Combine potatoes, mixed vegetables, green beans, bell pepper, picante sauce, broth, salt and sugar in slow cooker.

2. Cover; cook on LOW 8 hours or on HIGH 4 hours. Stir in parsley just before serving.

Makes 8 servings

Vegetable Lentil Soup

1 tablespoon olive oil

2 medium carrots, thinly sliced

½ cup chopped onion

4 cups vegetable broth

¾ cup dried lentils, rinsed

1 teaspoon salt

½ teaspoon ground cumin

⅛ teaspoon ground red pepper

1 medium tomato, seeded and diced

½ cup chopped roasted red peppers

1 tablespoon lemon juice or white wine vinegar

2 tablespoons chopped fresh cilantro

1. Heat oil in large saucepan or Dutch oven over medium-high heat. Add carrots and onion; cook and stir 5 minutes or until onion is translucent.

2. Add broth, lentils, salt, cumin and ground red pepper. Bring to a boil over high heat. Reduce heat; cover and simmer 45 minutes or until lentils are very tender.

3. Remove from heat; stir in tomato, roasted red peppers and lemon juice. Cover and let stand 5 minutes before serving. Sprinkle with cilantro.

—— **Makes 4 servings**

Butternut Squash and Okra Stew

8 ounces fresh okra *or*
   1 package (10 ounces) frozen cut okra, thawed

1 medium butternut squash

1 tablespoon olive oil

1½ cups chopped onions

1 clove garlic, minced

½ teaspoon ground cumin

½ teaspoon ground turmeric

¼ teaspoon ground cinnamon

¼ teaspoon ground red pepper

¼ teaspoon paprika

2 cups cubed unpeeled eggplant (optional)

2 cups sliced zucchini

1 medium carrot, sliced

1 can (8 ounces) tomato sauce

½ cup vegetable broth

1 can (about 15 ounces) chickpeas, rinsed and drained

1 medium tomato, chopped

⅓ cup raisins

Salt

Couscous (page 106)

Minced fresh parsley

1. Rinse okra under cold water. Cut into ¾-inch slices.

2. Peel butternut squash; trim off stem. Cut squash lengthwise into halves; discard seeds. Cut flesh into 1-inch pieces.

3. Heat oil in large saucepan over high heat. Add onions and garlic; cook and stir 5 minutes or until tender. Stir in cumin, turmeric, cinnamon, red pepper and paprika; cook and stir 2 to 3 minutes.

4. Add okra, butternut squash, eggplant, if desired, zucchini, carrot, tomato sauce and broth. Bring to a boil over high heat. Reduce heat to low. Simmer, uncovered, 5 minutes.

5. Add chickpeas, tomato and raisins; simmer, covered, 30 minutes. Season with salt.

6. Meanwhile, prepare couscous. Serve with stew; sprinkle with parsley.

—— **Makes 6 servings**

Hearty Mushroom and Barley Soup

9 cups vegetable broth

1 package (16 ounces) sliced mushrooms

1 onion, chopped

2 carrots, chopped

2 stalks celery, chopped

½ cup uncooked pearl barley

½ ounce dried porcini mushrooms

3 cloves garlic, minced

1 teaspoon salt

½ teaspoon dried thyme

½ teaspoon black pepper

Slow Cooker Directions

1. Combine broth, sliced mushrooms, onion, carrots, celery, barley, porcini mushrooms, garlic, salt, thyme and pepper in slow cooker.

2. Cover; cook on LOW 4 to 6 hours or until barley is tender.

Makes 8 servings

Chickpea and Butternut Squash Stew

1 tablespoon canola oil

1½ cups chopped onion

1 jalapeño pepper, seeded and minced

1 (1-inch) piece fresh ginger, peeled and minced

2 cloves garlic, minced

4 teaspoons ground cumin

1 teaspoon ground coriander

2 cups cubed peeled butternut squash, sweet potato or pumpkin

1 can (about 15 ounces) chickpeas, rinsed and drained

1 cup water

1 tablespoon soy sauce

1 can (about 13 ounces) coconut milk

Juice of 2 limes

¼ cup chopped fresh cilantro

Spinach leaves (optional)

1. Heat oil in medium saucepan over medium heat. Add onion, jalapeño, ginger and garlic; cook and stir 2 to 3 minutes or until onion is translucent. Add cumin and coriander; cook and stir 1 minute.

2. Add squash, chickpeas, water and soy sauce to saucepan. Bring to a boil. Reduce heat and simmer 15 minutes or until squash is tender.

3. Add coconut milk; cook and stir 2 to 3 minutes or until heated through. Stir in lime juice and cilantro. Garnish with spinach.

—— **Makes 2 to 4 servings**

BEANS & LEGUMES

Picante Pintos and Rice

2 cups dried pinto beans, rinsed and sorted

2 cups water

1 can (about 14 ounces) stewed tomatoes

1 cup chopped onion

¾ cup chopped green bell pepper

¼ cup sliced celery

4 cloves garlic, minced

½ jalapeño pepper, seeded and chopped

2 teaspoons dried oregano

2 teaspoons chili powder

1 teaspoon salt

½ teaspoon ground red pepper

2 cups chopped kale

3 cups hot cooked brown rice

1. Place beans in large saucepan; add water to cover by 2 inches. Bring to a boil over high heat; boil 2 minutes. Remove from heat; let stand, covered, 1 hour. Drain beans and return to saucepan.

2. Add 2 cups water, tomatoes, onion, bell pepper, celery, garlic, jalapeño, oregano, chili powder, salt and red pepper to saucepan; bring to a boil over high heat. Reduce heat to low. Simmer, covered, about 1½ hours or until beans are tender, stirring occasionally.

3. Gently stir kale into bean mixture. Simmer, uncovered, 30 minutes. (Beans will be very tender.) Serve over rice.

—— **Makes 8 servings**

Veggie Sausage and Bean Stew

2 cups fresh bread crumbs (see Note)

2 tablespoons olive oil, divided

1 package (about 16 ounces) meatless Italian or kielbasa sausage, cut into 2-inch pieces

1 leek, white and light green parts, cut in half and thinly sliced

1 large onion, quartered and cut into ¼-inch slices

1 teaspoon salt, divided

2 cloves garlic, minced

½ teaspoon dried thyme

½ teaspoon ground sage

¼ teaspoon paprika

¼ teaspoon ground allspice

¼ teaspoon black pepper

1 can (28 ounces) diced tomatoes

2 cans (about 15 ounces each) navy or cannellini beans, rinsed and drained

2 tablespoons whole grain mustard

Fresh thyme leaves (optional)

1. Preheat oven to 350°F. Combine bread crumbs and 1 tablespoon oil in medium bowl; mix well.

2. Heat remaining 1 tablespoon oil in large ovenproof skillet over medium-high heat. Add sausage; cook about 8 minutes or until browned, stirring occasionally. Remove to plate.

3. Add leek, onion and ½ teaspoon salt to skillet; cook 10 minutes or until vegetables are soft and beginning to brown, stirring occasionally. Add garlic; cook and stir 1 minute. Add dried thyme, sage, paprika, allspice and pepper; cook and stir 1 minute. Add tomatoes; cook 5 minutes, stirring occasionally. Stir in beans, mustard and remaining ½ teaspoon salt; bring to a simmer.

4. Return sausage to skillet, pushing down into bean mixture. Sprinkle with bread crumbs.

5. Bake about 25 minutes or until stew is hot and bread crumbs are lightly browned. Garnish with fresh thyme.

—— Makes 4 to 6 servings

Note: To make bread crumbs, cut 4 ounces of stale baguette or country bread into several pieces; place in a food processor. Pulse until coarse crumbs form.

Lentils with Walnuts >

1 cup dried brown lentils, rinsed

3 cups vegetable broth

1 small onion or large shallot, chopped

1 stalk celery, diced

1 large carrot, chopped

¼ teaspoon dried thyme

Salt and black pepper

¼ cup chopped walnuts

1. Combine lentils, broth, onion, celery, carrot, thyme and ½ teaspoon salt in large saucepan. Bring to a boil over medium-high heat. Reduce heat to medium-low; simmer 20 minutes or until lentils are tender. Drain any broth remaining in saucepan.

2. Season with additional salt and pepper. Spoon lentils into serving bowl and sprinkle with walnuts.

—— Makes 4 to 6 servings

Southwest Spaghetti Squash

1 spaghetti squash (about 3 pounds)

1 can (about 14 ounces) Mexican-style diced tomatoes

1 can (about 15 ounces) black beans, rinsed and drained

1 cup Monterey Jack-style vegan cheese alternative shreds, divided, (optional)

¼ cup finely chopped fresh cilantro

1 teaspoon ground cumin

¼ teaspoon garlic powder

Salt and black pepper

1. Preheat oven to 350°F.

2. Spray baking sheet and 1½-quart baking dish with nonstick cooking spray. Cut squash in half lengthwise; remove and discard seeds. Place squash, cut side down, on prepared baking sheet.

3. Bake 45 minutes or just until tender. Shred squash with fork; place in large bowl. (Use oven mitts to protect hands.) Add tomatoes, beans, ½ cup cheese alternative, if desired, cilantro, cumin and garlic powder. Season with salt and pepper to taste. Spoon into prepared baking dish; sprinkle with remaining ½ cup cheese alternative, if desired.

4. Bake 30 to 35 minutes or until heated through.

—— Makes 4 servings

Red, White and Black Bean Casserole

2 tablespoons olive oil

1 yellow or green bell pepper, cut into ½-inch strips

½ cup sliced green onions

1 can (14½ ounces) chunky-style salsa

1 can (4 ounces) diced green chiles, drained

1 package (1½ ounces) taco seasoning mix

2 tablespoons chopped fresh cilantro

½ teaspoon salt

2 cups cooked rice

1 can (19 ounces) white cannellini beans, rinsed and drained

1 can (about 15 ounces) red kidney beans, rinsed and drained

1 can (about 15 ounces) black beans, rinsed and drained

1 cup Cheddar-style vegan cheese alternative shreds, divided (optional)

1. Preheat oven to 350°F. Spray 13×9-inch baking dish with nonstick cooking spray.

2. Heat oil in large saucepan over medium-high heat. Add bell pepper and green onions; cook and stir about 5 minutes or until peppers are softened. Add salsa, chiles, taco seasoning mix, cilantro and salt; cook 5 minutes, stirring occasionally. Stir in rice and beans. Remove from heat; stir in ½ cup cheese alternative, if desired.

3. Spoon mixture into prepared baking dish. Sprinkle remaining ½ cup cheese alternative evenly over top, if desired. Cover and bake 30 to 40 minutes or until heated through.

—— **Makes 6 servings**

Corn and Bean Nachos

8 (6-inch) corn tortillas

1 tablespoon vegetable oil

1 cup chopped onion

1 tablespoon chili powder

2 teaspoons dried oregano

1 can (about 15 ounces) pinto beans or black beans, rinsed and drained

Salt and black pepper

1¼ cups Monterey Jack-style vegan cheese alternative shreds

¾ cup thawed frozen corn

1 jar (2 ounces) pimientos, drained

Sliced black olives

Pickled jalapeño pepper slices, drained

1. Preheat oven to 375°F. Sprinkle 1 tortilla with water to dampen; shake off excess water. Repeat with remaining tortillas. Cut each tortilla into 6 wedges. Arrange wedges in single layer on baking sheet or in two 9-inch pie plates. Bake 4 minutes. Rotate sheet. Bake 2 to 4 minutes or until chips are firm; do not allow chips to brown. Remove chips to plate to cool.

2. Heat oil in medium saucepan over medium-high heat. Add onion; cook and stir about 5 minutes or until tender. Add chili powder and oregano; cook and stir 1 minute. Remove from heat. Add beans and 2 tablespoons water; mash with fork or potato masher until blended but still chunky. Season with salt and black pepper to taste. Cover and cook over medium heat 6 to 8 minutes or until bubbly, stirring occasionally. Stir in additional water if beans become dry.

3. Sprinkle cheese alternative evenly over chips; top with beans. Combine corn and pimientos in small bowl; spoon over beans. Bake about 8 minutes or until cheese alternative melts. Sprinkle with olives and jalapeños.

—— Makes 4 servings

Beans and Spinach Bruschetta

1 can (about 15 ounces) Great Northern or cannellini beans, rinsed and drained

2 tablespoons water

4 tablespoons olive oil, divided

2 cloves garlic, minced

½ teaspoon salt, divided

½ teaspoon black pepper, divided

6 cups loosely packed spinach, finely chopped

1 tablespoon red wine vinegar

1 whole grain baguette, cut into 16 slices

1. Place beans and 2 tablespoons water in food processor; process until smooth. Transfer to medium bowl.

2. Heat 1 tablespoon oil in large skillet over medium-low heat. Add garlic; cook and stir 1 minute. Remove from heat; add ¼ teaspoon salt and ¼ teaspoon pepper. Stir into beans.

3. Heat 1 tablespoon oil in same skillet over medium heat. Add spinach; cook 2 to 3 minutes or until wilted. Stir in vinegar, remaining ¼ teaspoon salt and ¼ teaspoon pepper. Remove from heat.

4. Preheat grill or broiler. Brush baguette slices with remaining 2 tablespoons oil. Grill until bread is golden brown and crisp. Top with bean mixture and spinach. Serve immediately.

—— **Makes 16 servings**

Mexican-Style Lentil and Black Bean Salad

Dressing

- ½ cup chopped sun-dried tomatoes packed in oil, drained
- 3 tablespoons balsamic vinegar
- 12 fresh basil leaves
- 1 teaspoon sugar
- ½ teaspoon chili powder
- ¼ teaspoon salt
- ¼ teaspoon black pepper
- ½ cup olive oil

Salad

- ½ cup dried lentils, rinsed
- 2 large red bell peppers, halved and seeded
- 1 can (about 15 ounces) black beans, rinsed and drained
- 1½ cups thawed frozen corn
- ½ cup finely chopped onion
- ¼ cup chopped fresh parsley
- Tortilla chips (optional)

1. For dressing, place tomatoes, vinegar, basil, sugar, chili powder, salt and black pepper in food processor; process until almost smooth. With motor running, gradually add oil; process until well combined. Refrigerate until ready to serve.

2. Place lentils in medium saucepan; cover with 2 inches of water. Bring to a boil over medium heat. Reduce heat to low; cover and simmer 35 minutes or until lentils are tender. Drain.

3. Preheat broiler. Place bell peppers on foil-lined broiler pan. Broil 4 inches from heat 15 to 20 minutes or until blackened on all sides, turning peppers every 5 minutes. Place blackened peppers in paper or plastic bag. Close bag; set aside to cool about 15 minutes. Place cooled peppers on cutting board. Peel off skins with paring knife. Lay peppers flat; slice lengthwise into ¼-inch strips. Cut strips into 2-inch pieces.

4. Combine beans, lentils, bell peppers, corn, onion and parsley in large bowl. Pour dressing over bean mixture; mix well. Cover and refrigerate 2 to 3 hours for flavors to blend. Serve with tortilla chips, if desired.

—— Makes 4 to 6 servings

Vegetable Pilaf with Spiced Bean Sauce

- 2 cups uncooked basmati rice or brown rice
- 2 tablespoons vegetable oil, divided
- ½ cup chopped leek (white and light green parts)
- 1 serrano or jalapeño pepper, minced
- ½ teaspoon ground ginger
- ¼ teaspoon ground turmeric
- 1 bay leaf
- 1 can (about 15 ounces) kidney beans, rinsed and drained
- 1⅓ cups vegetable broth
- Salt and black pepper
- 1 pound broccoli, cut into florets
- 2 carrots, chopped
- ½ teaspoon ground cinnamon
- ¼ cup peanuts

1. Cook rice according to package directions; keep warm.

2. For sauce, heat 1 tablespoon oil in medium skillet over medium heat until hot. Add leek, serrano pepper, ginger, turmeric and bay leaf; cook and stir 3 to 5 minutes or until leek is tender. Add beans and broth; bring to a boil over high heat. Reduce heat to low; simmer 5 minutes. Remove and discard bay leaf.

3. Transfer bean mixture to food processor; process until chunky. Return to skillet; cook over low heat 2 to 3 minutes or until heated through. Season to taste with salt and black pepper; keep warm.

4. Heat remaining 1 tablespoon oil in large skillet over medium-high heat. Add broccoli and carrots; cook and stir 5 minutes or until tender. Stir in cinnamon. Stir carrot mixture into rice; season to taste with salt and pepper.

5. Serve bean sauce over rice; sprinkle with peanuts.

—— Makes 6 servings

Chickpea Patties

3 tablespoons boiling water

1 tablespoon ground flaxseed

1 can (about 15 ounces) chickpeas, rinsed and drained

⅓ cup chopped carrots

⅓ cup panko bread crumbs

¼ cup chopped fresh parsley

¼ cup chopped onion

1 teaspoon minced garlic

1 teaspoon grated lemon peel

½ teaspoon salt

½ teaspoon black pepper

2 tablespoons vegetable or canola oil

Hamburger buns (optional)

Tomato slices, lettuce leaves and salsa (optional)

1. Combine boiling water and flaxseed in small bowl. Let stand until cool; refrigerate until ready to use.

2. Place chickpeas, carrots, panko, parsley, onion, garlic, lemon peel, salt and pepper in food processor; process until blended. Add flaxseed mixture; pulse until blended. Shape mixture into four patties.

3. Heat 1 tablespoon oil in large nonstick skillet over medium heat. Add patties; cook 4 to 5 minutes or until bottoms are browned. Add remaining 1 tablespoon to skillet; flip patties and cook 4 to 5 minutes or until browned. Serve burgers on buns with tomato, lettuce and salsa, if desired.

—— Makes 4 servings

Meal Idea: Serve these patties alongside Pineapple Ginger Slaw with Quinoa (page 14).

Fruity Baked Beans

2 tablespoons olive oil

¼ cup chopped onion

2 cans (16 ounces each) vegetarian baked beans

1 can (about 11 ounces) mandarin oranges, drained

1 can (about 8 ounces) pineapple chunks in juice, drained

½ cup chopped green bell pepper

¼ cup ketchup

2 tablespoons packed brown sugar

½ teaspoon salt (optional)

Dash hot pepper sauce

1. Preheat oven to 375°F. Spray 2-quart baking dish with nonstick cooking spray.

2. Heat oil in small skillet over medium heat. Add onion; cook and stir until translucent. Combine onion, beans, oranges, pineapple, bell pepper, ketchup and brown sugar in large bowl. Taste and season with salt, if desired. Add hot pepper sauce to taste. Spread evenly in prepared baking dish.

3. Bake 30 to 35 minutes or until bubbly.

—— Makes 6 to 8 servings

Southwestern Salad

Salad

- **1 can (about 15 ounces) black beans, rinsed and drained**
- **1½ cups thawed frozen corn**
- **1½ cups chopped seeded tomatoes**
- **½ cup thinly sliced green onions**
- **¼ cup minced fresh cilantro**
- **1 jalapeño pepper, seeded and minced (optional)**

Dressing

- **½ cup vegetable oil**
- **2 tablespoons red wine vinegar**
- **1 teaspoon salt**
- **½ teaspoon black pepper**

1. Combine beans, corn, tomatoes, green onions, cilantro and jalapeño, if desired, in large bowl.
2. Whisk oil, vinegar, salt and black pepper in small bowl. Pour over salad; stir gently to combine. Serve immediately or refrigerate until ready to serve.

—— **Makes 6 servings**

GRAINS & COUSCOUS

Quinoa Tabbouleh

1 cup uncooked tricolor quinoa *or* ½ cup *each* red and white quinoa

2 cups water

2 teaspoons salt, divided

2 cups chopped fresh tomatoes (red, orange or a combination)

1 cucumber, quartered lengthwise and thinly sliced

¼ cup olive oil

3 tablespoons lemon juice

½ teaspoon black pepper

1 red or orange bell pepper, chopped

½ cup minced fresh parsley

1. Rinse quinoa in fine-mesh strainer under cold water. Combine 2 cups water, quinoa and 1 teaspoon salt in medium saucepan. Bring to a boil over high heat. Reduce heat to low; cover and simmer 10 to 15 minutes or until quinoa is tender and water is absorbed. Transfer to large bowl; cool to room temperature.

2. Meanwhile, combine tomatoes, cucumber and remaining 1 teaspoon salt in medium bowl. Let stand 20 minutes.

3. For dressing, whisk oil, lemon juice and black pepper in small bowl until well blended.

4. Stir bell pepper, parsley and cucumber mixture with any accumulated juices into quinoa mixture. Add dressing; mix well. Taste and season with additional salt and black pepper, if desired.

—— **Makes 6 to 8 servings**

Note: For a heartier dish, stir in 1 can (15 ounces) of chickpeas, rinsed and drained, in step 4.

Mujadara

- 1 cup dried brown lentils, rinsed
- ¼ cup plus 1 tablespoon olive oil, divided
- 3 sweet onions, thinly sliced
- 2½ teaspoons salt, divided
- 1½ teaspoons ground cumin
- 1 teaspoon ground allspice
- 1 cinnamon stick
- 1 bay leaf
- ⅛ to ¼ teaspoon ground red pepper
- ¾ cup uncooked long grain white rice, rinsed and drained
- 3 cups vegetable broth or water
- 1 cucumber (optional)
- 1 cup sour cream or vegan sour cream alternative (optional)

1. Place lentils in medium saucepan; cover with 1 inch of water. Bring to a boil over medium-high heat. Reduce heat to medium-low; simmer 10 minutes. Drain and rinse under cold water.

2. Meanwhile, heat ¼ cup oil in large saucepan or Dutch oven. Add onions and 1 teaspoon salt; cook and stir 15 minutes or until golden and parts are crispy. Remove most of onions to small bowl, leaving about ½ cup in saucepan.*

3. Add remaining 1 tablespoon oil to saucepan with onions; heat over medium-high heat. Add cumin, allspice, cinnamon stick, bay leaf and red pepper; cook and stir 30 seconds. Add rice; cook and stir 2 to 3 minutes or until rice is lightly toasted. Add broth, lentils and 1 teaspoon salt; bring to a boil. Reduce heat to low; cover and cook about 15 minutes or until broth is absorbed and rice and lentils are tender. Remove saucepan from heat. Place clean kitchen towel over top of saucepan; replace lid and let stand 5 to 10 minutes.

4. For cucumber sauce, if desired, peel cucumber and trim ends. Grate cucumber on large holes of box grater; squeeze out excess liquid. Place in medium bowl; stir in sour cream and remaining ½ teaspoon salt. Serve lentils and rice with reserved onions and cucumber sauce, if desired.

*If desired, continue to cook reserved onions in a medium skillet over medium heat until dark golden brown.

—— **Makes 4 to 6 servings**

Mixed Grain Tabbouleh

1 cup uncooked long grain
   brown rice

3 cups vegetable broth,
   divided

½ cup uncooked bulgur
   wheat

1 cup chopped tomatoes

½ cup minced green onions

¼ cup fresh mint, chopped

¼ cup fresh basil, chopped

¼ cup fresh oregano,
   chopped

3 tablespoons lemon juice

3 tablespoons olive oil

½ teaspoon salt

½ teaspoon black pepper

1. Combine rice and 2 cups broth in medium saucepan. Bring to a boil over medium-high heat. Reduce heat to low. Cover and simmer 35 to 45 minutes or until broth is absorbed and rice is tender.

2. Combine bulgur and remaining 1 cup broth in small saucepan. Bring to a boil over medium-high heat. Reduce heat to low. Cover and simmer 15 minutes or until broth is absorbed and bulgur is fluffy.

3. Combine tomatoes, green onions, chopped herbs, lemon juice, oil, salt and pepper in large bowl. Stir in rice and bulgur. Cool to room temperature before serving.

—— **Makes 4 servings**

Mediterranean Barley-Bean Salad

⅔ cup uncooked pearl barley

3 cups asparagus pieces

2 cans (about 15 ounces each) dark red kidney beans, rinsed and drained

2 tablespoons chopped fresh mint

¼ cup lemon juice

¼ cup Italian salad dressing

¼ teaspoon salt

¼ teaspoon black pepper

¼ cup dry-roasted sunflower seeds

1. Cook barley according to package directions. Add asparagus during last 5 minutes of cooking; drain. Transfer to large bowl; refrigerate at least 2 hours.

2. Stir beans and mint into barley mixture. Whisk lemon juice, salad dressing, salt and pepper in small bowl until well blended. Add to barley mixture; toss to coat. Sprinkle with sunflower seeds.

—— Makes 4 servings

Millet Pilaf

1 tablespoon olive oil

½ onion, finely chopped

½ red bell pepper, finely chopped

1 carrot, finely chopped

2 cloves garlic, minced

1 cup uncooked millet

3 cups water

Grated peel and juice of 1 lemon

¾ teaspoon salt

¼ teaspoon black pepper

2 tablespoons chopped fresh parsley (optional)

1. Heat oil in medium saucepan over medium heat. Add onion, bell pepper, carrot and garlic; cook and stir 5 minutes or until softened. Add millet; cook and stir 5 minutes or until lightly toasted.

2. Stir in water, lemon peel, lemon juice, salt and black pepper; bring to a boil. Reduce heat to low; cover and simmer 30 minutes or until water is absorbed and millet is tender. Cover and let stand 5 minutes. Fluff with fork. Sprinkle with parsley, if desired.

—— Makes 6 servings

Bulgur Pilaf with Caramelized Onions and Kale >

1 tablespoon olive oil

1 small onion, cut into thin wedges

1 clove garlic, minced

2 cups chopped kale

2 cups vegetable broth

¾ cup medium grain bulgur

½ teaspoon salt

¼ teaspoon black pepper

1. Heat oil in large skillet over medium heat. Add onion; cook about 8 minutes, stirring frequently or until softened and lightly browned. Add garlic; cook and stir 1 minute. Add kale; cook and stir about 1 minute or until kale is wilted.

2. Stir in broth, bulgur, salt and pepper. Bring to a boil. Reduce heat; cover and simmer 12 minutes or until liquid is absorbed and bulgur is tender.

—— **Makes 4 servings**

Fruited Rice

½ cup slivered almonds

2 tablespoons vegetable oil

1 medium onion, chopped

1 medium green bell pepper, diced

2¼ cups vegetable broth

1 cup uncooked basmati rice

1 cinnamon stick

¼ teaspoon turmeric

1 can (8 ounces) pineapple chunks in juice, drained

½ cup raisins

½ teaspoon ground nutmeg

1. Preheat oven to 350°F. Spread almonds in single layer on baking sheet. Bake 8 to 10 minutes or until golden brown, stirring frequently. Transfer almonds to plate. Cool completely.

2. Heat oil in large saucepan over medium-high heat. Add onion and bell pepper; cook and stir about 5 minutes or until vegetables are tender.

3. Add broth, rice, cinnamon stick and turmeric. Bring to a boil over medium-high heat. Reduce heat to low; cover and simmer 15 to 18 minutes or until rice is tender and liquid is absorbed. Remove and discard cinnamon stick.

4. Stir in pineapple, almonds, raisins and nutmeg.

—— **Makes 6 to 8 servings**

Sizzling Rice Cakes with Mushrooms and Bell Peppers

¾ cup uncooked short grain rice*

1¾ cups water, divided

1 can (about 14 ounces) vegetable broth

1 tablespoon soy sauce

2 teaspoons sugar

2 teaspoons red wine vinegar

2 tablespoons cornstarch

3 tablespoons peanut oil

1½ teaspoons finely chopped fresh ginger

2 cloves garlic, thinly sliced

1 red bell pepper, cut into short strips

1 green bell pepper, cut into short strips

8 ounces button mushrooms, quartered

4 ounces fresh shiitake or other exotic mushrooms, sliced

1 teaspoon toasted sesame oil

Vegetable oil for frying

Short grain rice works best in this recipe because of its sticky texture when cooked. It may be labeled sweet or glutinous rice.

1. Rinse rice in fine-mesh sieve under cold water to remove excess starch. Combine rice and 1½ cups water in medium saucepan. Bring to a boil over medium-high heat. Reduce heat to low; cover and simmer 15 to 20 minutes or until water is absorbed. Let cool.

2. Combine broth, soy sauce, sugar and vinegar in medium bowl. Stir cornstarch into remaining ¼ cup water in small cup until smooth.

3. Heat peanut oil in wok over medium-high heat. Add ginger and garlic; stir-fry 10 seconds. Add bell peppers and mushrooms; stir-fry 4 to 5 minutes or until peppers are crisp-tender and mushrooms are softened. Transfer to plate.

4. Add broth mixture to wok and bring to a boil. Stir cornstarch mixture; add to wok. Cook and stir until sauce boils and thickens slightly. Stir in sesame oil; return vegetables to wok. Remove from heat; keep warm.

5. Shape rice into 12 (2-inch) cakes with dampened hands.

6. Heat 2 to 3 inches of vegetable oil in large skillet over medium-high heat to 375°F; adjust heat to maintain temperature. Add 4 rice cakes; cook 2 to 3 minutes or until puffed and golden, turning once. Remove with slotted spatula to paper towels. Repeat with remaining rice cakes.

7. Place rice cakes in serving bowl. Stir vegetable mixture; pour over rice cakes.

—— **Makes 4 to 6 servings**

Buckwheat with Zucchini and Mushrooms

2 tablespoons olive oil

1 cup sliced mushrooms

1 medium zucchini, cut into ½-inch pieces

1 medium onion, chopped

1 clove garlic, minced

¾ cup uncooked buckwheat

¼ teaspoon dried thyme

¼ teaspoon salt

⅛ teaspoon black pepper

1¼ cups vegetable broth

1. Heat oil in large nonstick skillet over medium heat. Add mushrooms, zucchini, onion and garlic; cook and stir 7 to 10 minutes or until vegetables are tender. Add buckwheat, thyme, salt and pepper; cook and stir 2 minutes.

2. Add broth; bring to a boil. Cover; reduce heat to low. Cook 10 to 13 minutes or until liquid is absorbed and buckwheat is tender. Remove from heat; let stand, covered, 5 minutes.

—— **Makes 6 servings**

Couscous >

1 tablespoon olive oil

1 medium onion, finely chopped

1 stalk celery, finely chopped

1 clove garlic, minced

2¼ cups vegetable broth

1 box (10 ounces) couscous (about 1½ cups uncooked)

Salt and black pepper

1. Heat oil in large saucepan over medium-high heat. Add onion and celery; cook and stir 4 minutes or until celery has softened and onion is translucent. Add garlic; cook and stir about 1 minute or until fragrant.

2. Add broth; bring to a boil. Stir in couscous. Reduce heat to low; cover and simmer 5 minutes or until broth is absorbed. Remove from heat; fluff couscous with fork. Season with salt and pepper to taste.

—— Makes about 5 cups

Baked Spanish Rice and Barley

1 tablespoon vegetable oil

½ cup chopped onion

½ cup chopped green bell pepper

2 cloves garlic, minced

1 cup coarsely chopped seeded tomatoes

1 cup vegetable broth

½ cup uncooked rice

½ cup water

3 tablespoons uncooked quick-cooking barley

¼ teaspoon salt

¼ teaspoon black pepper

1. Preheat oven to 350°F. Spray 1½-quart baking dish with nonstick cooking spray.

2. Heat oil in medium saucepan over medium heat. Add onion, bell pepper and garlic; cook and stir 5 minutes or until tender. Stir in tomatoes, broth, rice, water, barley, salt and black pepper. Bring to a boil over high heat.

3. Pour into prepared baking dish. Cover and bake 25 to 30 minutes or until rice and barley are tender and liquid is absorbed. Fluff with fork.

—— Makes 4 servings

Slow Cooker Vegetarian Paella

2 tablespoons olive oil

1 medium onion, chopped

1 medium red bell pepper, chopped

2 cloves garlic, minced

1½ cups uncooked converted rice

2 cans (about 14 ounces each) vegetable broth

½ cup dry white wine

½ teaspoon crushed saffron threads, smoked paprika or ground turmeric

¾ teaspoon salt

¼ teaspoon red pepper flakes

1 can (about 15 ounces) chickpeas, rinsed and drained

1 package (11 ounces) frozen artichoke hearts, thawed

½ cup frozen peas, thawed

Slow Cooker Directions

1. Heat oil in medium skillet over medium heat. Add onion, bell pepper and garlic; cook and stir 5 minutes or until softened. Transfer to slow cooker. Stir in rice, broth, wine, saffron, salt and red pepper flakes. Cover; cook on LOW 3 hours.

2. Add chickpeas, artichoke hearts and peas to slow cooker; do not stir. Cover; cook on LOW about 30 minutes or until rice is tender and liquid is absorbed. Stir before serving.

—— **Makes 6 servings**

Barley and Swiss Chard Skillet Casserole

1 cup water

1 cup chopped red bell pepper

1 cup chopped green bell pepper

¾ cup uncooked quick-cooking barley

⅛ teaspoon garlic powder

⅛ teaspoon red pepper flakes

2 cups packed coarsely chopped Swiss chard

1 can (about 15 ounces) navy beans, rinsed and drained

1 cup quartered cherry tomatoes

¼ cup chopped fresh basil

1 tablespoon olive oil

2 tablespoons Italian-seasoned dry bread crumbs

1. Preheat broiler.

2. Bring water to a boil in large ovenproof skillet. Add bell peppers, barley, garlic powder and red pepper flakes; cover and cook over low heat 10 minutes or until liquid is absorbed. Remove from heat; stir in chard, beans, tomatoes, basil and oil. Sprinkle with bread crumbs.

3. Broil 2 minutes or until golden.

—— **Makes 4 servings**

Quinoa and Mango Salad

1 cup uncooked quinoa

2 cups water

2 cups cubed peeled mangoes (about 2 large mangoes)

½ cup sliced green onions

½ cup dried cranberries

2 tablespoons chopped fresh parsley

¼ cup olive oil

1½ tablespoons white wine vinegar

1 teaspoon Dijon mustard

½ teaspoon salt

⅛ teaspoon black pepper

1. Place quinoa in fine-mesh strainer; rinse under cold water. Combine quinoa and 2 cups water in medium saucepan; bring to a boil over high heat. Reduce heat to low; cover and simmer 10 to 12 minutes or until quinoa is tender and water is absorbed. Stir quinoa; let stand, covered, 15 minutes. Transfer to large bowl; cover and refrigerate at least 1 hour.

2. Add mangoes, green onions, cranberries and parsley to quinoa; mix well.

3. Combine oil, vinegar, mustard, salt and pepper in small bowl; whisk until blended. Pour over quinoa mixture; mix until well blended.

—— **Makes 6 servings**

Tip: This salad can be made several hours ahead and refrigerated. Allow it to stand at room temperature for at least 30 minutes before serving.

Spiced Chickpeas and Couscous

1 can (about 14 ounces) vegetable broth

1 teaspoon ground coriander

½ teaspoon ground cardamom

½ teaspoon ground turmeric

½ teaspoon hot pepper sauce

¼ teaspoon salt

⅛ teaspoon ground cinnamon

1 cup julienned or shredded carrots

1 can (about 15 ounces) chickpeas, rinsed and drained

1 cup frozen green peas

1 cup quick-cooking couscous

2 tablespoons chopped fresh mint or parsley

1. Combine broth, coriander, cardamom, turmeric, hot pepper sauce, salt and cinnamon in large saucepan; bring to a boil over high heat. Add carrots; reduce heat and simmer 5 minutes.

2. Add chickpeas and green peas; return to a simmer. Simmer 2 minutes.

3. Stir in couscous. Cover; remove from heat. Let stand 5 minutes or until liquid is absorbed. Fluff with fork. Sprinkle with mint.

—— Makes 6 servings

Quinoa and Roasted Vegetables

2 sweet potatoes, cut into ½-inch-thick slices

1 eggplant, peeled and cut into ½-inch cubes

1 medium tomato, cut into wedges

1 green bell pepper, sliced

1 onion, cut into wedges

3 tablespoons olive oil, divided

1 teaspoon salt, divided

¼ teaspoon black pepper

¼ teaspoon ground red pepper

1 cup uncooked quinoa

2 cloves garlic, minced

½ teaspoon dried thyme

¼ teaspoon dried marjoram

2 cups vegetable broth

1. Preheat oven to 450°F. Line large baking sheet with foil; spray with nonstick cooking spray.

2. Combine sweet potatoes, eggplant, tomato, bell pepper and onion on prepared baking sheet. Drizzle with 2 tablespoons oil. Sprinkle with ½ teaspoon salt, black pepper and ground red pepper; toss to coat. Spread vegetables in single layer. Roast 20 to 30 minutes or until vegetables are browned and tender.

3. Meanwhile, place quinoa in fine-mesh strainer; rinse well under cold water. Heat remaining 1 tablespoon oil in medium saucepan over medium heat. Add garlic, thyme and marjoram; cook and stir 1 to 2 minutes. Add quinoa; cook and stir 2 to 3 minutes.

4. Stir in broth and remaining ½ teaspoon salt; bring to a boil over high heat. Reduce heat to low. Cover and simmer 15 to 20 minutes or until quinoa is tender and water is absorbed. Transfer quinoa to large bowl; gently stir in roasted vegetables.

—— Makes 6 servings

VEGETABLES

Spicy Pickled Relish

8 serrano or jalapeño
    peppers, thinly sliced

2 banana peppers, sliced

3 cups cauliflower florets

2 carrots, thinly sliced

½ cup salt

1½ cups olive oil

1½ cups white vinegar

3 cloves garlic, thinly sliced

1 teaspoon dried oregano

1. Layer peppers, cauliflower and carrots in large jar or large covered bowl or container. Sprinkle with salt; fill with water to cover. Cover and refrigerate overnight.

2. Drain and thoroughly rinse vegetables under cold water. Return vegetables to jar. Pour oil and vinegar over vegetables. Add garlic and oregano; cover and shake or stir until well coated. Marinate in refrigerator at least 8 hours.

—— **Makes 6 cups**

Curried Cauliflower and Brussels Sprouts

2 pounds cauliflower florets

12 ounces brussels sprouts, cleaned and cut in half lengthwise

⅓ cup olive oil

2½ tablespoons curry powder

½ teaspoon salt

½ teaspoon black pepper

½ cup chopped fresh cilantro

1. Preheat oven to 400°F. Line large baking sheet with foil.

2. Combine cauliflower, brussels sprouts and oil in large bowl; toss to coat. Sprinkle with curry powder, salt and pepper; toss to coat. Spread in single layer on prepared baking sheet.

3. Roast 20 to 25 minutes or until golden brown and tender, stirring after 15 minutes. Sprinkle with cilantro; toss until blended.

—— Makes 10 servings

Crispy Smashed Potatoes

1 tablespoon plus
    ½ teaspoon salt, divided

3 pounds unpeeled small
    red potatoes (2 inches
    or smaller)

4 tablespoons olive oil,
    divided

¼ teaspoon black pepper

1. Fill large saucepan three-fourths full with water; add 1 tablespoon salt. Bring to a boil over high heat. Add potatoes; boil about 20 minutes or until potatoes are tender when pierced with tip of sharp knife. Drain potatoes; set aside until cool enough to handle.

2. Preheat oven to 450°F. Brush baking sheet with 2 tablespoons oil. Working with one potato at a time, smash with hand or bottom of measuring cup to about ½-inch thickness. Arrange smashed potatoes in single layer on prepared baking sheet. Brush with remaining 2 tablespoons oil; sprinkle with remaining ½ teaspoon salt and pepper.

3. Bake 30 to 40 minutes or until bottoms of potatoes are golden brown. Turn potatoes; bake 10 minutes or until browned on bottoms and potatoes are crispy.

—— **Makes about 6 servings**

Stuffed Portobellos

2 teaspoons olive oil

½ cup diced red bell pepper

½ cup diced onion

¼ teaspoon dried thyme

Salt and black pepper

⅔ cup panko bread crumbs

⅔ cup diced fresh tomatoes or drained canned diced tomatoes

¼ cup nutritional yeast or grated Parmesan cheese

¼ cup chopped fresh parsley

4 portobello mushroom caps, gills and stems removed

1. Preheat oven to 375°F.

2. Heat oil in medium skillet over medium-high heat. Add bell pepper and onion; cook and stir 5 minutes or until tender. Season with thyme, salt and black pepper.

3. Combine vegetable mixture, panko, tomatoes, nutritional yeast and parsley in medium bowl. Place mushrooms, cap sides down, in shallow baking dish. Mound vegetable mixture on mushrooms.

4. Bake 15 minutes or until mushrooms are tender and filling is golden brown.

———— **Makes 4 servings**

Creamy Slab Potatoes

¼ cup olive oil

1 teaspoon salt

½ teaspoon dried rosemary

½ teaspoon dried thyme

¼ teaspoon black pepper

2½ pounds Yukon Gold potatoes (6 to 8 potatoes), peeled and cut crosswise into 1-inch slices

1 cup water

3 cloves garlic, smashed

1. Preheat oven to 500°F.

2. Combine oil, salt, rosemary, thyme and pepper in 13×9-inch baking pan (do not use glass); mix well. Add potatoes; toss to coat. Spread in single layer.

3. Bake 15 minutes. Turn potatoes; bake 15 minutes. Add water and garlic to pan; bake 15 minutes. Remove to serving plate; pour any liquid remaining in pan over potatoes.

——— **Makes 4 servings**

Cornmeal-Crusted Cauliflower Steaks

½ cup cornmeal

¼ cup all-purpose flour

1 teaspoon salt

1 teaspoon dried sage

½ teaspoon garlic powder

Black pepper

½ cup oatmilk

2 heads cauliflower

4 tablespoons olive oil

Barbecue sauce (optional)

1. Preheat oven to 400°F. Line baking sheet with parchment paper.

2. Combine cornmeal, flour, salt, sage and garlic powder in shallow bowl or baking pan. Season with pepper. Pour oatmilk into another shallow bowl.

3. Turn cauliflower stem side up on cutting board. Trim away leaves, leaving stem intact. Slice through stem into 3 slices. Trim off excess florets from end slices, creating flat "steaks." Repeat with remaining cauliflower. Reserve extra cauliflower for another use.

4. Dip cauliflower slices into oatmilk to coat both sides. Place in cornmeal mixture; pat onto all sides of cauliflower. Place on prepared baking sheet; drizzle evenly with oil.

5. Bake 40 minutes or until cauliflower is tender. Serve with barbecue sauce for dipping, if desired.

—— **Makes 4 servings**

Meal Idea: Serve with Fruity Baked Beans (page 86) and Colorful Coleslaw (page 9).

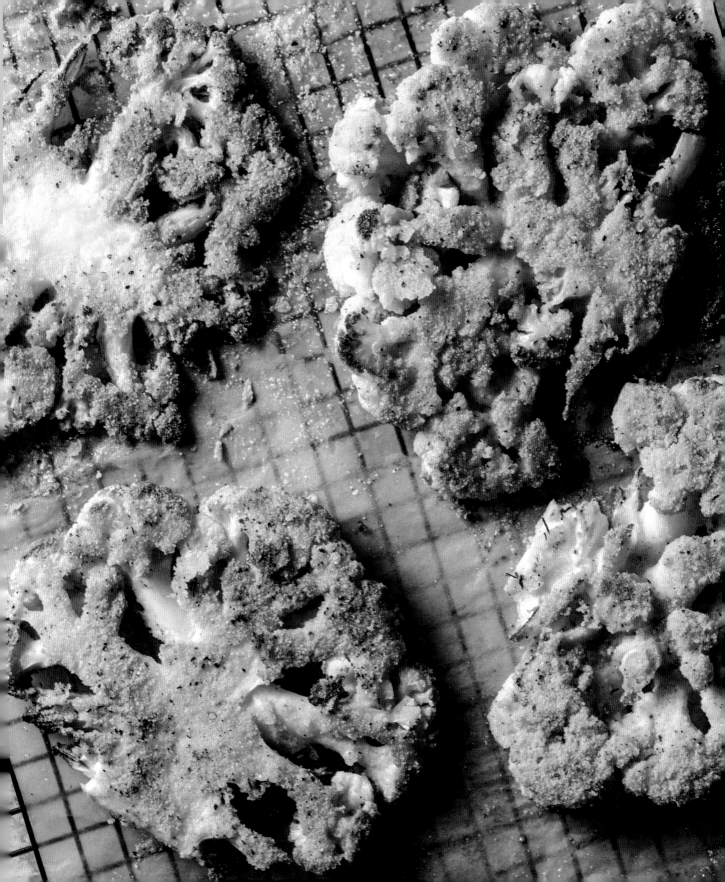

Barley, Hazelnut and Pear Stuffed Squash

3 to 3¼ cups vegetable broth, divided

1 teaspoon salt, divided

1 cup uncooked pearl barley

2 acorn squash, halved and seeded

3 tablespoons olive oil, divided

¼ plus ⅛ teaspoon black pepper, divided

½ cup water

1 small onion, chopped

1 stalk celery, chopped

1 large ripe pear, cut into ½-inch dice

¼ teaspoon dried thyme

½ cup chopped toasted hazelnuts*

To toast hazelnuts, cook in medium skillet over medium heat 3 to 4 minutes or until lightly browned and fragrant, stirring frequently.

1. Bring 3 cups broth and ¼ teaspoon salt to a boil in large saucepan over high heat. Stir in barley. Reduce heat to low. Simmer 45 minutes or until barley is tender. Remove from heat; set aside.

2. Meanwhile, preheat oven to 350°F. Brush cut sides of squash with 1 tablespoon oil. Season with ½ teaspoon salt and ¼ teaspoon pepper. Place cut sides down on sheet pan; add ½ cup water to pan. Roast about 45 minutes or until squash is tender when pierced with fork. Place squash on serving plates.

3. Heat 1 tablespoon oil in large skillet over medium heat. Add onion and celery; cook and stir 5 minutes or until softened. Add remaining 1 tablespoon oil. Stir in pear; cook and stir 5 minutes. Add barley, remaining ¼ teaspoon salt, thyme and ⅛ teaspoon pepper. If mixture is dry, add remaining ¼ cup broth. Stir in hazelnuts. Mound into squash halves.

—— **Makes 4 servings**

Peppery Green Beans

1 pound whole green beans,
    ends trimmed

1 medium onion, cut into
    ½-inch wedges

1 medium red bell pepper,
    cut into ½-inch slices

2 tablespoons olive oil

2 teaspoons vegan
    Worcestershire sauce or
    soy sauce

1 clove garlic, minced

½ teaspoon salt

½ teaspoon black pepper

1. Preheat oven to 450°F. Line baking sheet with foil. Place beans, onion and bell pepper on prepared baking sheet.

2. Combine oil, Worcestershire sauce, garlic, ½ teaspoon salt and ½ teaspoon black pepper in small bowl; mix well. Pour half of oil mixture over vegetables; toss to coat. Spread vegetables in single layer.

3. Bake 20 to 25 minutes or until vegetables begin to brown, stirring every 5 minutes. Add remaining oil mixture; toss to coat. Season with additional salt and pepper, if desired.

—— **Makes 4 servings**

Chili Stuffed Potatoes

4 medium russet potatoes

1 tablespoon vegetable oil

1 cup chopped onion

½ cup chopped green bell pepper

2 cloves garlic, minced

1 can (about 15 ounces) kidney beans, rinsed and drained

1 can (about 14 ounces) diced tomatoes

1 can (4 ounces) diced mild green chiles

¼ cup chopped fresh cilantro or parsley

2 teaspoons chili powder

1 teaspoon ground cumin

½ teaspoon salt

¼ teaspoon ground red pepper

1. Preheat oven to 350°F. Scrub potatoes; pierce with fork. Bake 1¼ to 1½ hours or until tender.

2. Meanwhile, heat oil in medium saucepan over medium heat. Add onion, bell pepper and garlic; cook and stir 5 minutes or until vegetables are tender. Stir in beans, tomatoes, chiles, cilantro, chili powder, cumin, salt and red pepper. Bring to a boil over high heat. Reduce heat to medium-low. Cover and simmer 8 minutes, stirring occasionally.

3. Gently roll potatoes to loosen pulp. Cut crisscross slit in each potato. Place potatoes on serving plates. Press potato ends to open; spoon bean mixture over potatoes.

—— **Makes 4 servings**

Whole Roasted Cauliflower

6 tablespoons olive oil, divided

1 head cauliflower, leaves trimmed

½ teaspoon plus ⅛ teaspoon salt, divided

Black pepper

¼ cup water

¾ cup panko bread crumbs

¼ cup shredded Parmesan cheese or nutritional yeast

1 clove garlic, minced

¼ teaspoon dried oregano

¼ teaspoon dried sage

⅛ teaspoon red pepper flakes

1. Preheat oven to 400°F. Line 13×9-inch baking pan with foil.

2. Rub 4 tablespoons oil all over cauliflower, 1 tablespoon at a time. Sprinkle with ½ teaspoon salt and black pepper. Place in prepared baking pan; add ¼ cup water to pan. Roast 45 minutes, adding additional water if pan is dry.

3. Combine panko, cheese, garlic, oregano, sage, red pepper flakes and remaining ⅛ teaspoon salt in small bowl. Stir in remaining 2 tablespoons oil. Remove pan from oven and carefully pat panko mixture all over and under cauliflower. Bake 15 minutes or until panko is browned and cauliflower is tender. Cut into wedges to serve.

—— **Makes 4 to 6 servings**

Meal Idea: Serve with Spiced Chickpeas and Couscous (page 114) and Kale Salad with Cherries and Avocados (page 34).

Roasted Carrots, Beets and Red Onions

2 medium beets, peeled, cut into ½-inch wedges and patted dry with paper towels

4 carrots, cut crosswise into 2-inch pieces

1 medium red onion, cut into ½-inch wedges

2 tablespoons olive oil

1 teaspoon salt

½ teaspoon dried oregano

¼ teaspoon black pepper

1. Preheat oven to 425°F. Line large baking sheet with foil; spray with nonstick cooking spray.

2. Combine beets, carrots and onion in large bowl. Add oil, salt, oregano and pepper; toss gently to coat. Pour vegetables onto prepared baking sheet; arrange in single layer.

3. Bake 15 minutes. Stir vegetables; bake 10 minutes or until vegetables are tender when pierced with a fork.

——— **Makes 4 servings**

Grilled Spaghetti Squash with Black Beans and Zucchini

1 spaghetti squash (about 2 pounds)

2 medium zucchini, cut lengthwise into ¼-inch-thick slices

1 tablespoon vegetable oil

2 cups chopped seeded tomatoes

1 can (about 15 ounces) black beans, rinsed and drained

2 tablespoons chopped fresh basil

2 tablespoons olive oil

2 tablespoons red wine vinegar

1 clove garlic, minced

½ teaspoon salt

1. Prepare grill for direct cooking. Pierce spaghetti squash in several places with fork. Place in center of large piece of heavy-duty foil. Bring two long sides of foil together above squash; fold down in series of locked folds, allowing room for heat circulation and expansion. Fold short ends up and over again. Press folds firmly to seal foil packet.

2. Grill squash, covered, over medium heat 45 minutes to 1 hour or until easily depressed with back of long-handled spoon, turning a quarter turn every 15 minutes. Remove squash from grill; let stand in foil 10 to 15 minutes.

3. Meanwhile, brush both sides of zucchini slices with vegetable oil. Grill, uncovered, over medium heat 4 minutes or until tender, turning once. Cut into bite-size pieces.

4. Remove spaghetti squash from foil; cut in half and remove seeds. Separate squash into strands with two forks; place on large serving plate.

5. Combine zucchini, tomatoes, beans and basil in medium bowl. Whisk olive oil, vinegar, garlic and salt in small bowl until well blended. Add to vegetables; toss gently to coat. Serve over spaghetti squash.

—— **Makes 4 servings**

Collard Greens

4 bunches collard greens, stemmed, washed and torn into bite-size pieces

2 cups water

½ medium red bell pepper, cut into strips

⅓ medium green bell pepper, cut into strips

¼ cup olive oil

¼ teaspoon salt

¼ teaspoon black pepper

1. Place collard greens, water, bell peppers, oil, salt and black pepper in large saucepan; bring to a boil. Reduce heat to low.

2. Simmer 1 to 1½ hours or until tender.

—— **Makes 10 servings**

Meal Idea: Serve with Cornmeal-Crusted Cauliflower Steaks (page 128) or Whole Roasted Cauliflower (page 136) and Fruited Rice (page 100).

Curried Cauliflower Rice and Vermicelli

1 tablespoon canola or
    vegetable oil

½ cup finely chopped onion

1 clove garlic, minced

1 teaspoon curry powder

½ teaspoon ground
    coriander

¼ teaspoon salt

⅓ cup uncooked long
    grain rice

⅓ cup broken vermicelli
    (1-inch pieces)

1 cup apple juice

½ cup water

3 cups cauliflower florets
    (½-inch pieces)

3 tablespoons golden
    raisins

1. Heat oil in large skillet over medium heat. Add onion and garlic; cook and stir 2 minutes. Add curry powder, coriander and salt; cook and stir 1 minute. Stir in rice and vermicelli until coated with spices. Remove from heat.

2. Bring apple juice and water to a boil in small saucepan; pour over rice and vermicelli mixture. Bring mixture to a boil over high heat. Reduce heat to low; cover and simmer 15 minutes.

3. Set cauliflower and raisins on top of rice mixture. Cover and simmer about 7 minutes or until water is absorbed. Stir cauliflower and raisins into rice mixture. Remove from heat; let stand, covered, 5 minutes or until cauliflower is crisp-tender. Fluff with fork before serving.

—— **Makes 4 servings**

Dragon Tofu

1 package (14 to 16 ounces) firm tofu, drained

¼ cup soy sauce

1 tablespoon creamy peanut butter

1 medium zucchini

1 medium yellow squash

1 medium red bell pepper

2 teaspoons peanut or vegetable oil

½ teaspoon hot chili oil

2 cloves garlic, minced

2 cups packed torn fresh spinach

Hot cooked rice

¼ cup coarsely chopped cashews or peanuts

1. Press tofu lightly between paper towels; cut into ¾-inch triangles or squares. Place in single layer in shallow dish. Whisk soy sauce into peanut butter in small bowl until smooth. Pour mixture over tofu; stir gently to coat. Let stand at room temperature 20 minutes.

2. Meanwhile, cut zucchini and yellow squash lengthwise into ¼-inch-thick slices; cut each slice into 2-inch strips. Cut bell pepper into 2-inch strips.

3. Heat peanut oil and chili oil in large wok or skillet over medium-high heat. Add garlic, zucchini, yellow squash and bell pepper; stir-fry 3 minutes. Add tofu mixture; cook 2 minutes or until tofu is heated through and sauce is slightly thickened, stirring occasionally. Stir in spinach; remove from heat. Serve over rice; sprinkle with cashews.

===== Makes 2 servings

PASTA & NOODLES

Sesame Noodles

- 1 package (16 ounces) uncooked spaghetti
- 6 tablespoons soy sauce
- 5 tablespoons toasted sesame oil
- 3 tablespoons sugar
- 3 tablespoons rice vinegar
- 2 tablespoons vegetable oil
- 3 cloves garlic, minced
- 1 teaspoon grated fresh ginger
- ½ teaspoon sriracha
- 2 green onions, sliced
- 1 red bell pepper
- 1 cucumber
- 1 carrot
  Sesame seeds (optional)

1. Cook spaghetti in large saucepan of salted boiling water according to package directions for al dente. Drain, reserving 1 tablespoon pasta cooking water.

2. Whisk soy sauce, sesame oil, sugar, vinegar, vegetable oil, garlic, ginger, sriracha and reserved pasta water in large bowl. Stir in noodles and green onions. Let stand at least 30 minutes or until noodles have cooled to room temperature and most of sauce is absorbed, stirring occasionally.

3. Meanwhile, cut bell pepper into thin strips. Peel cucumber and carrot and shred with julienne peeler into long strands, or cut into thin strips. Stir into noodles. Serve at room temperature or refrigerate until ready to serve. Top with sesame seeds, if desired.

—— Makes 6 to 8 servings

Lentils with Pasta

1 cup dried lentils

1 cup dried split peas

1 tablespoon olive oil

1 onion, chopped

2 tablespoons tomato paste

2 cloves garlic, minced

1 teaspoon salt

¼ teaspoon black pepper

1 can (about 14 ounces) diced tomatoes

3 cups water

12 ounces uncooked short pasta (elbow macaroni, small shells, ditalini or similar)

1. Place lentils and split peas in medium bowl; cover with water. Let stand at least 10 minutes.

2. Heat oil in large saucepan or Dutch oven over medium heat. Add onion; cook and stir 7 to 10 minutes or until onion is lightly browned. Add tomato paste, garlic, salt and pepper; cook and stir 1 minute. Add tomatoes and 3 cups water; bring to a boil.

3. Drain lentils and split peas and add to saucepan. Reduce heat to medium-low; cover and simmer about 40 minutes or until lentils and split peas are tender.

4. Meanwhile, cook pasta in large saucepan of salted boiling water according to package directions for al dente. Drain and add to lentil mixture; mix well.

—— **Makes 6 to 8 servings**

Roasted Fennel and Spaghetti

2 bulbs fennel, trimmed, cored and sliced ¼-inch thick

2 carrots, peeled and quartered

1 tablespoon plus 2 teaspoons olive oil, divided

Salt and black pepper

1 cup fresh bread crumbs

2 cloves garlic, minced

8 ounces uncooked spaghetti or vermicelli

2 tablespoons fresh lemon juice

2 tablespoons chopped fresh oregano

1. Preheat oven to 400°F. Place fennel and carrots on large baking sheet. Drizzle with 1 teaspoon oil and sprinkle lightly with salt and pepper (about ¼ teaspoon each). Toss to coat; spread in single layer.

2. Bake 30 minutes or until vegetables are tender and well browned, stirring once or twice. When carrots are cool enough to handle, cut diagonally into 1-inch pieces.

3. Meanwhile, heat 1 tablespoon oil in medium skillet over medium heat. Add bread crumbs and garlic; cook and stir about 3 minutes or until bread is toasted. Transfer to small bowl; season with ¼ teaspoon salt.

4. Cook pasta in large saucepan of salted boiling water according to package directions for al dente. Drain and return to saucepan. Stir in lemon juice and remaining 1 teaspoon oil. Divide pasta among serving bowls. Top with vegetables, bread crumbs and oregano.

—— Makes 2 to 4 servings

Fried Vegetable Rice Noodles

½ cup soy sauce

⅓ cup sugar

¼ cup lime juice

2 fresh red Thai chiles *or*
   1 large jalapeño pepper,
   finely chopped

8 ounces thin rice noodles
   (rice vermicelli)

¼ cup vegetable oil

8 ounces firm tofu, drained
   and cut into triangles

1 jicama (8 ounces), peeled
   and chopped *or* 1 can
   (8 ounces) sliced water
   chestnuts, drained

2 medium sweet potatoes
   (1 pound), peeled and
   cut into ¼-inch-thick
   slices

2 large leeks, cut into
   ¼-inch-thick slices

¼ cup chopped dry-roasted
   peanuts

2 tablespoons chopped
   fresh mint

2 tablespoons chopped
   fresh cilantro

1. Combine soy sauce, sugar, lime juice and chiles in small bowl until well blended; set aside.

2. Place rice noodles in medium bowl. Cover with hot water; let stand 15 minutes or until soft. Drain well; cut into 3-inch lengths.

3. Meanwhile, heat oil in large skillet over medium-high heat. Add tofu; cook 4 minutes per side or until golden brown. Remove with slotted spatula to paper towel-lined baking sheet.

4. Add jicama to skillet; stir-fry 5 minutes or until lightly browned. Remove to baking sheet. Stir-fry sweet potatoes in batches until tender and browned; remove to baking sheet. Add leeks to skillet; stir-fry 1 minute; remove to baking sheet.

5. Stir soy sauce mixture; add to skillet. Cook until sugar dissolves. Add noodles; toss to coat. Gently stir in tofu, vegetables, peanuts, mint and cilantro.

—— **Makes 4 servings**

Szechuan Cold Noodles

8 ounces uncooked vermicelli, broken in half, or Chinese egg noodles

3 tablespoons rice vinegar

3 tablespoons soy sauce

2 tablespoons peanut or vegetable oil

1 clove garlic, minced

1 teaspoon minced fresh ginger

1 teaspoon toasted sesame oil

½ teaspoon crushed Szechuan peppercorns or red pepper flakes

¼ cup coarsely chopped fresh cilantro (optional)

¼ cup chopped peanuts

1. Cook noodles in large saucepan of salted boiling water according to package directions for al dente; drain.

2. Combine vinegar, soy sauce, peanut oil, garlic, ginger, sesame oil and peppercorns in large bowl; mix well. Add hot cooked noodles; toss to coat. Sprinkle with cilantro, if desired, and peanuts. Serve at room temperature or chilled.

—— Makes 4 servings

Szechuan Vegetable Noodles: Add 1 cup chopped peeled cucumber, ½ cup chopped red bell pepper, ½ cup sliced green onions and an additional 1 tablespoon soy sauce.

Puttanesca with Angel Hair Pasta

2 tablespoons olive oil

3 cloves garlic, minced

2 tablespoons tomato paste

2 cans (about 14 ounces each) diced tomatoes

1 teaspoon dried oregano

1 teaspoon dried basil

Salt and black pepper

1 can (14 ounces) tomato sauce

½ cup pitted Greek olives, coarsely chopped

2 tablespoons drained capers

½ to 1½ teaspoons red pepper flakes

1 package (16 ounces) uncooked angel hair or vermicelli pasta

1. Heat oil in large skillet over medium-low heat. Add garlic; cook and stir 30 seconds or until lightly browned. Add tomato paste; cook 2 minutes, stirring constantly.

2. Stir in tomatoes; cook and stir to break up tomatoes. Add oregano, basil, salt and pepper. Increase heat to medium; cook, stirring occasionally about 30 minutes or until tomatoes break down and mixture becomes saucy. Turn heat to medium-low and add tomato sauce, olives, capers and red pepper flakes; simmer 10 minutes.

3. Meanwhile, cook pasta in large saucepan of salted boiling water according to package directions for al dente. Drain and add to skillet with sauce; toss gently to coat.

—— **Makes 4 to 6 servings**

Summer Spaghetti

1 pound plum tomatoes,
    coarsely chopped

1 medium onion, chopped

⅓ cup chopped fresh parsley

6 pitted green olives,
    chopped

2 cloves garlic, minced

2 tablespoons finely
    shredded fresh basil

2 teaspoons drained capers

½ teaspoon paprika

¼ teaspoon dried oregano

1 tablespoon red wine
    vinegar

½ cup olive oil

1 package (16 ounces)
    uncooked spaghetti

1. Combine tomatoes, onion, parsley, olives, garlic, basil, capers, paprika and oregano in medium bowl; mix well. Drizzle with vinegar. Add oil; stir until well blended. Cover and refrigerate at least 6 hours or overnight.

2. Cook pasta in large saucepan of salted boiling water according to package directions for al dente; drain. Toss hot pasta with tomato mixture. Serve immediately.

—— Makes 4 to 6 servings

Pasta with Avocado and Bell Pepper

3 cups uncooked multigrain or whole wheat penne or rotini pasta

1 ripe avocado, diced

1 red or green bell pepper, diced

½ cup oil-packed sun-dried tomatoes, drained and chopped

½ cup chopped fresh basil

2 green onions, chopped

2 tablespoons olive oil

¼ teaspoon salt

¼ teaspoon black pepper

1. Cook pasta in large saucepan of salted boiling water according to package directions for al dente. Drain and return to saucepan.

2. Combine avocado, bell pepper, tomatoes, basil, green onions and oil in large bowl; mix gently. Add hot pasta; toss until blended. Season with salt and black pepper.

—— Makes 4 servings

Soba Stir-Fry

8 ounces uncooked soba (buckwheat) noodles

1 tablespoon olive oil

2 cups sliced shiitake mushrooms

1 medium red bell pepper, cut into thin strips

2 whole dried red chiles *or* ¼ teaspoon red pepper flakes

1 clove garlic, minced

2 cups shredded napa cabbage

½ cup vegetable broth

2 tablespoons tamari or soy sauce

1 tablespoon rice wine or dry sherry

2 teaspoons cornstarch

1 package (14 to 16 ounces) firm tofu, drained and cut into 1-inch cubes

Salt and black pepper

2 green onions, thinly sliced

1. Bring large saucepan of salted water to a boil. Add noodles; return to a boil. Reduce heat to low; cook 3 minutes or until tender. Drain and rinse under cold water to cool.

2. Heat oil in large skillet or wok over medium-high heat. Add mushrooms, bell pepper, dried chiles and garlic; cook and stir 3 minutes or until mushrooms are tender. Add cabbage; cover and cook 2 minutes or until cabbage is wilted.

3. Whisk broth, tamari and rice wine into cornstarch in small bowl until smooth. Stir sauce into vegetable mixture. Cook 2 minutes or until sauce is thickened.

4. Stir tofu and noodles into vegetable mixture; toss gently until heated through. Season with salt and black pepper. Sprinkle with green onions. Serve immediately.

—— **Makes 4 servings**

Penne with Spring Vegetables

3 cups uncooked whole wheat or multigrain penne

¼ cup olive oil

½ cup chopped onion

2 cloves garlic, minced

1 pound asparagus, cut into 1-inch pieces

2½ cups halved cherry tomatoes (12 ounces)

2 cups diced yellow squash

¾ cup vegetable broth

¼ teaspoon salt

¼ teaspoon black pepper

1½ cups marinara sauce

6 fresh basil leaves, cut into thin strips

1. Cook pasta in large saucepan of salted boiling water according to package directions for al dente; drain.

2. Heat oil in large saucepan over medium heat. Add onion and garlic; cook 3 minutes, stirring constantly. Add asparagus; cook and stir 4 minutes. Add tomatoes and squash; cook and stir 3 minutes or until tomatoes are softened. Add broth. Reduce heat; simmer 6 minutes or until asparagus is tender. Season with salt and pepper.

3. Add pasta, sauce and basil to tomato mixture; toss to combine.

—— Makes 4 servings

Spaghetti Mediterranean

1½ pounds fresh tomatoes (about 4 large)

12 ounces uncooked spaghetti

¼ cup olive oil

2 cloves garlic, minced

½ cup chopped fresh parsley

12 pitted green olives, sliced

1 tablespoon drained capers

1 tablespoon chopped fresh basil *or* ½ teaspoon dried basil

½ teaspoon dried oregano

½ teaspoon salt

¼ teaspoon red pepper flakes

1. Bring large saucepan of water to a boil. Add tomatoes; cook 1 minute to loosen skins. Immediately drain tomatoes and rinse under cold water. Peel, seed and coarsely chop tomatoes.

2. Cook pasta in large saucepan of salted boiling water according to package directions for al dente; drain.

3. Meanwhile, heat oil in medium skillet over medium-high heat. Add garlic; cook and stir 45 seconds or just until garlic begins to color. Stir in tomatoes, parsley, olives, capers, basil, oregano, salt and red pepper flakes; cook and stir 10 minutes over medium-high heat until most of liquid has evaporated and sauce is slightly thickened. Pour sauce over pasta; toss lightly. Serve immediately.

—— **Makes 4 servings**

Pesto Fettuccine

1 pound uncooked whole wheat fettuccine

1 cup packed fresh basil leaves

½ cup pine nuts or almonds, toasted*

2 cloves garlic

½ teaspoon salt

¼ teaspoon black pepper

¼ cup plus 1 tablespoon olive oil, divided

*To toast pine nuts, cook in medium skillet over medium heat 3 to 4 minutes or until lightly browned and fragrant, stirring frequently.

1. Cook pasta in large saucepan of salted boiling water according to package directions for al dente; drain.

2. Meanwhile, place basil, pine nuts, garlic, salt and pepper in food processor; drizzle with 1 tablespoon oil. Process about 10 seconds or until coarsely chopped. With motor running, drizzle in remaining ¼ cup oil. Process about 30 seconds or until almost smooth. Toss with hot cooked pasta in large bowl.

—— **Makes 4 servings**

Note: Pesto can be made 1 week in advance. Transfer to a covered container and store in the refrigerator. Pesto also makes a great sandwich spread or topping for crostini.

Baked Veggie Mac and Nooch

1½ cups uncooked elbow macaroni

1 cup chopped onion

1 cup chopped red or green bell pepper

¾ cup chopped celery

¾ cup nutritional yeast

¼ cup all-purpose flour

1½ teaspoons salt

¼ teaspoon garlic powder

¼ teaspoon onion powder

1½ cups unsweetened oatmilk or other dairy-free milk

1 teaspoon prepared yellow mustard

3 drops hot pepper sauce (optional)

½ teaspoon paprika

1. Preheat oven to 350°F. Spray 12×8-inch baking dish with nonstick cooking spray. Cook pasta in large saucepan of salted boiling water according to package directions for al dente; add onion, bell pepper and celery during last 5 minutes of cooking. Drain, reserving ½ cup pasta cooking water; return pasta and vegetables to saucepan.

2. Meanwhile, combine nutritional yeast, flour, salt, garlic powder and onion powder in medium saucepan. Whisk in oatmilk and reserved pasta water over medium heat until smooth. Add mustard and hot pepper sauce, if desired. Continue whisking 10 minutes or until mixture thickens to desired consistency. Pour over pasta and vegetables; mix well.

3. Spread mixture in prepared baking dish; sprinkle with paprika. Bake 15 to 20 minutes or until heated through.

—— **Makes 4 to 6 servings**

MAINS & BOWLS

Ginger Tofu Bowl

7 tablespoons soy sauce,
    divided

2 teaspoons minced fresh
    ginger

1 teaspoon toasted
    sesame oil

1 package (14 to 16 ounces)
    firm tofu, drained and
    cut into ½-inch cubes

1 cup uncooked brown rice

½ seedless cucumber, thinly
    sliced

¼ teaspoon salt

¼ teaspoon sugar

¼ cup rice vinegar

1 teaspoon olive oil

1 package (8 ounces)
    sliced cremini or white
    mushrooms

1 cup thawed frozen shelled
    edamame

2 carrots, julienned or
    shredded

4 green onions, thinly sliced

    Sesame seeds

    Pickled ginger

1. Combine 6 tablespoons soy sauce, ginger and sesame oil in large resealable food storage bag or large shallow bowl. Add tofu; seal bag and turn to coat. Refrigerate 2 hours or overnight.

2. Prepare rice according to package directions.

3. Meanwhile, place cucumbers in shallow bowl. Sprinkle with salt and sugar; toss to coat. Add vinegar; mix well.

4. Heat 1 teaspoon olive oil in medium skillet. Add mushrooms; cook and stir 5 minutes or until mushrooms are tender and lightly browned. Remove from heat; stir in remaining 1 tablespoon soy sauce.

5. Divide rice among four bowls. Arrange tofu, mushrooms, cucumbers, edamame and carrots over rice. Top with green onions, sesame seeds and pickled ginger.

—— **Makes 4 servings**

Mexican Cauliflower and Bean Skillet

1 teaspoon olive oil

3 cups coarsely chopped cauliflower

¾ teaspoon salt

½ medium yellow onion, chopped

1 green bell pepper, chopped

1 clove garlic, minced

1 teaspoon chili powder

¾ teaspoon ground cumin

Pinch ground red pepper

1 can (about 15 ounces) black beans, rinsed and drained

1 cup (4 ounces) shredded Cheddar-Jack cheese or Cheddar-style vegan cheese alternative

Salsa

1. Heat oil in large skillet over medium-high heat. Add cauliflower and salt; cook and stir 5 minutes. Add onion, bell pepper, garlic, chili powder, cumin and ground red pepper; cook and stir 5 minutes or until cauliflower is tender. Stir in beans; cook until beans are heated through. Remove from heat.

2. Sprinkle with cheese; fold gently and let stand until melted. Serve with salsa.

—— **Makes 4 to 6 servings**

Serving Suggestion: Serve over brown rice or with warm corn tortillas.

Red Beans and Rice

1 pound dried red kidney
    beans

1 tablespoon plus
    1 teaspoon salt, divided

Pickled Carrots and
    Cucumbers (page 179)

2 tablespoons olive oil

2 onions, chopped

3 stalks celery, chopped

1 green bell pepper,
    chopped

4 cloves garlic, minced

4 cups vegetable broth

1 teaspoon liquid smoke

1 bay leaf

2 teaspoons Italian
    seasoning

½ teaspoon black pepper

¼ teaspoon ground red
    pepper

½ cup water

Hot cooked brown rice

Sliced avocado

Hot pepper sauce

1. Place beans in large bowl. Cover with water and stir in 1 tablespoon salt. Soak 8 hours or overnight. Meanwhile, prepare pickled carrots and cucumbers.

2. Heat oil in large saucepan over medium-high heat. Add onions; cook and stir 5 minutes. Stir in remaining 1 teaspoon salt. Add celery, bell pepper and garlic; cook and stir 5 minutes or until vegetables are tender.

3. Drain beans; add to saucepan with broth, liquid smoke, bay leaf, Italian seasoning, black pepper and red pepper. Bring to a boil. Reduce heat; simmer, partially covered, 45 minutes.

4. Remove 2 cups bean mixture to medium bowl; let stand 15 minutes to cool slightly. Place in blender or food processor and add ½ cup water; blend until smooth. Stir into beans; continue to cook until beans are tender. Taste and season with additional salt, if desired. Serve with rice, pickled carrots and cucumbers, avocado and hot pepper sauce.

—— **Makes 6 servings**

Pickled Carrots and Cucumbers

2 carrots, peeled

1 cucumber

¼ cup water

2 tablespoons sugar

1 tablespoon salt

1 teaspoon peppercorns

2 cloves garlic, smashed

¼ teaspoon dried dill

2 bay leaves

1½ cups white vinegar

1. Thinly slice carrots into coins. Very thinly slice cucumber (⅟₁₆-inch slices) with a mandoline if you have one. Place carrots and cucumbers in 1-quart jar.

2. Combine water, sugar, salt, peppercorns, garlic, dill and bay leaves in small saucepan. Cook over medium heat just until salt and sugar are dissolved. Pour over vegetables in jar. Add enough vinegar to cover. Seal jar and refrigerate at least 2 hours. Can be made a few days in advance.

Pumpkin Curry

1 tablespoon vegetable oil

1 package (14 to 16 ounces) firm tofu, drained, patted dry and cut into 1-inch cubes

¼ cup Thai red curry paste

2 cloves garlic, minced

1 can (15 ounces) pumpkin purée

1 can (about 13 ounces) unsweetened coconut milk

1 cup vegetable broth or water

1½ teaspoons salt

1 teaspoon sriracha sauce

4 cups cut-up fresh vegetables (broccoli, cauliflower, red bell pepper and/or sweet potato)

½ cup peas

Hot cooked rice

¼ cup shredded fresh basil (optional)

1. Heat oil in wok or large skillet over high heat. Add tofu; stir-fry 5 minutes or until lightly browned. Add curry paste and garlic; cook and stir 1 minute or until tofu is coated.

2. Add pumpkin, coconut milk, broth, salt and sriracha; bring to a boil. Stir in vegetables. Reduce heat to medium; cover and simmer 20 minutes or until vegetables are tender.

3. Stir in peas; cook 1 minute or until heated through. Serve over rice; top with basil, if desired.

—— **Makes 4 servings**

Black Bean and Tempeh Burritos

2 teaspoons olive oil

½ cup chopped onion

½ cup chopped green bell pepper

2 cloves garlic, minced

2 teaspoons chili powder

2 cans (about 14 ounces each) stewed tomatoes

1 teaspoon dried oregano

½ teaspoon dried coriander

1 can (about 15 ounces) black beans, rinsed and drained

4 ounces tempeh, diced

¼ cup minced onion

¼ teaspoon black pepper

½ teaspoon ground cumin

8 (6-inch) flour tortillas

1. For sauce, heat oil in large nonstick skillet over medium heat. Add chopped onion, bell pepper and garlic; cook and stir 5 minutes or until onion is tender. Add chili powder; cook 1 minute. Add tomatoes, oregano and coriander; cook 15 minutes, stirring frequently.

2. Preheat oven to 350°F. Spray 13×9-inch baking dish with nonstick cooking spray. Place beans in medium bowl; mash well with fork. Stir in tempeh, minced onion, black pepper and cumin. Stir in ¼ cup sauce.

3. Soften tortillas if necessary.* Spread ⅓ cup bean mixture down center of each tortilla. Roll up tortillas; place in single layer in prepared baking dish. Top with remaining sauce. Bake 15 minutes or until heated through.

*To soften tortillas, wrap stack of tortillas in foil. Heat in preheated 350°F oven about 10 minutes or until softened.

—— **Makes 4 servings**

Vegan Spinach-Artichoke Lasagna

1 tablespoon olive oil

1 cup chopped onion

3 cloves garlic, chopped

¼ cup tomato paste

¼ cup dry white wine

1 can (28 ounces) crushed tomatoes

1 teaspoon salt

1 teaspoon sugar

1 teaspoon dried oregano

Not Ricotta (recipe follows)

1 can (14 ounces) artichoke hearts, drained and chopped

1 package (10 ounces) frozen chopped spinach, thawed and squeezed dry

9 no-boil lasagna noodles

2 cups mozzarella-style vegan cheese alternative shreds

2 roasted bell peppers, chopped

1. For sauce, heat oil in large saucepan over medium-high heat. Add onion; cook and stir 5 minutes or until onion is tender. Add garlic; cook and stir 30 seconds. Stir in tomato paste; cook and stir 1 minute. Stir in wine; cook 30 seconds. Add tomatoes with juice, salt, sugar and oregano; break up tomatoes with spoon. Reduce heat to low; partially cover and simmer 30 minutes.

2. Meanwhile, prepare not ricotta. Combine artichokes and spinach in small bowl.

3. Preheat oven to 350°F. Spray 13×9-inch baking dish with nonstick cooking spray. Spread ½ cup sauce in dish; arrange three noodles over sauce. Spread half of not ricotta over noodles; top with artichoke mixture, half of cheese shreds and ½ cup sauce. Repeat layers of noodles and not ricotta; top with roasted peppers, remaining 3 noodles, sauce and cheese shreds.

4. Cover with greased foil; bake 45 minutes. Remove foil; bake 15 minutes. Let stand 10 minutes before serving.

—— Makes 8 servings

Not Ricotta: Drain 1 package (14 to 16 ounces) firm tofu and pat dry. Crumble into large bowl. Add 1 cup silken tofu, ½ cup chopped fresh parsley, 2 teaspoons salt, 2 teaspoons lemon juice, 1 teaspoon sugar and 1 teaspoon black pepper; mix well. Refrigerate until needed. Drain liquid before using.

Barbecue Seitan Skewers

1 package (8 ounces)
   seitan, cubed

½ cup barbecue sauce,
   divided

1 red bell pepper, cut into
   12 pieces

1 green bell pepper, cut into
   12 pieces

12 cremini mushrooms

1 zucchini, cut into 12 pieces

1. Place seitan in medium bowl. Add ¼ cup barbecue sauce; stir to coat. Marinate in refrigerator 30 minutes. Soak four bamboo skewers in water 20 minutes.

2. Oil grid. Prepare grill for direct cooking. Thread seitan, bell peppers, mushrooms and zucchini onto skewers.

3. Grill skewers, covered, over medium-high heat 8 minutes or until seitan is hot and glazed with sauce, brushing with some of remaining sauce and turning occasionally.

—— **Makes 4 servings**

Fried Tofu with Vegetables

1 package (14 to 16 ounces) firm tofu

½ cup soy sauce, divided

1 cup all-purpose flour

¾ teaspoon salt, divided

⅛ teaspoon black pepper
Vegetable oil for frying

1 pound broccoli florets

2 carrots, halved lengthwise and sliced crosswise

2 cups snow peas

3 tablespoons water

1 teaspoon cornstarch

3 tablespoons plum sauce

2 tablespoons lemon juice

2 teaspoons sugar

1 teaspoon minced fresh ginger

⅛ to ¼ teaspoon red pepper flakes

1. Drain tofu; cut into ¾-inch cubes. Gently mix tofu and ¼ cup soy sauce in shallow bowl; let stand 5 minutes. Combine flour, ½ teaspoon salt and black pepper in another shallow bowl. Working with a few pieces at a time, toss tofu cubes in flour mixture to coat.

2. Heat 1½ inches of oil in wok or Dutch oven. Test heat by dropping 1 tofu cube into oil; it should brown in 1 minute. Fry tofu cubes in small batches until browned. Remove from oil with slotted spoon and drain on paper towels.

3. Pour off all but 1 tablespoon oil from wok. Add broccoli, carrots, snow peas and remaining ¼ teaspoon salt; cook and stir over medium-high heat 6 to 8 minutes or until vegetables are crisp-tender.

4. Stir water into cornstarch in small bowl until smooth. Add remaining ¼ cup soy sauce, plum sauce, lemon juice, sugar, ginger and red pepper flakes; mix well. Add sauce to wok with tofu. Stir-fry 1 to 2 minutes or until sauce is thickened and tofu and vegetables are glazed.

—— **Makes 6 servings**

Four-Pepper Black Bean Fajitas

1 can (about 15 ounces) black beans, rinsed and drained

¼ cup water

3 tablespoons olive oil, divided

2 tablespoons lime juice

1 canned chipotle pepper in adobo sauce

1 clove garlic, minced

¼ teaspoon salt

1 red bell pepper, cut into strips

1 green bell pepper, cut into strips

1 yellow bell pepper, cut into strips

2 onions, cut into ¼-inch wedges

8 (8-inch) flour tortillas

¼ cup chopped fresh cilantro

Salsa and guacamole (optional)

1. Combine beans, water, 2 tablespoons oil, lime juice, chipotle pepper, garlic and salt in food processor or blender; process until smooth. Place in medium saucepan; cook over medium-low heat until heated through. Keep warm.

2. Heat remaining 1 tablespoon oil in large skillet over medium-high heat. Add bell peppers and onions; cook and stir 12 minutes or until beginning to brown.

3. Heat tortillas according to package directions.

4. To serve, divide bean mixture among tortillas; top with bell pepper mixture. Sprinkle with cilantro and serve with salsa and guacamole, if desired.

—— **Makes 4 servings**

Note: You can use 3 bell peppers in any color combination in this recipe, or even substitute 1 or 2 poblano peppers for one of the bell peppers.

Lentil Rice Curry

2 tablespoons olive oil

1 cup sliced green onions

3 cloves garlic, minced

2 tablespoons minced fresh ginger

2 teaspoons curry powder

½ teaspoon ground cumin

½ teaspoon ground turmeric

3 cups water

1 can (about 14 ounces) diced tomatoes

½ teaspoon salt

1 cup dried red lentils, rinsed

1 large head cauliflower, broken into florets

1 tablespoon lemon juice

Fragrant Basmati Rice

2 cups apple juice

¾ cup water

½ teaspoon salt

1½ cups uncooked white basmati rice

2 thin slices fresh ginger

1 cinnamon stick

1. Heat oil in large saucepan over medium heat. Add green onions, garlic, minced ginger, curry powder, cumin and turmeric; cook and stir 5 minutes. Add 3 cups water, tomatoes and ½ teaspoon salt; bring to a boil over high heat.

2. Stir in lentils. Reduce heat to low; cover and simmer 35 to 40 minutes or until lentils are tender. Add cauliflower and lemon juice. Cover and simmer 8 to 10 minutes or until cauliflower is tender.

3. Meanwhile for rice, bring juice, ¾ cup water and ½ teaspoon salt to a boil in medium saucepan. Add rice, ginger slices and cinnamon stick. Reduce heat to low; cover and cook about 20 minutes or until liquid is absorbed and rice is tender. Remove and discard ginger slices and cinnamon stick. Serve with lentil curry.

—— Makes 6 servings

Broccoli-Tofu Stir-Fry

2 cups uncooked rice

1 can (about 14 ounces) vegetable broth, divided

3 tablespoons cornstarch

2 tablespoons soy sauce

1 teaspoon packed brown sugar

1 teaspoon toasted sesame oil

1 package (14 to 16 ounces) extra firm tofu, drained and pressed*

1 tablespoon peanut oil

1 tablespoon minced fresh ginger

3 cloves garlic, minced

3 cups broccoli florets

2 cups sliced mushrooms

½ cup chopped green onions

1 red bell pepper, seeded and cut into strips

Prepared Szechuan sauce (optional)

*Place tofu on cutting board on several layers of paper towels. Cover with additional paper towels and weigh down with another cutting board, heavy plate or saucepan. Let stand 15 to 20 minutes.

1. Cook rice according to package directions.

2. Whisk ¼ cup vegetable broth, cornstarch, soy sauce, sugar and sesame oil in small bowl until smooth and well blended; set aside. Cut tofu into 1-inch cubes; set aside.

3. Heat peanut oil in wok or large nonstick skillet over medium heat. Add ginger and garlic; stir-fry 2 to 3 minutes or until fragrant but not browned.

4. Increase heat to medium-high. Add remaining vegetable broth, broccoli, mushrooms, green onions and bell pepper to wok; stir-fry 5 minutes or until vegetables are crisp-tender. Add tofu; stir-fry 2 minutes.

5. Stir soy sauce mixture; add to wok. Stir-fry until sauce boils and is thickened. Serve over rice with Szechuan sauce, if desired.

—— **Makes 6 servings**

Tofu Satay with Peanut Sauce

Satay

1 package (14 to 16 ounces) firm tofu, drained and pressed*

⅓ cup water

⅓ cup soy sauce

1 tablespoon toasted sesame oil

1 teaspoon minced garlic

1 teaspoon minced fresh ginger

24 white button mushrooms, trimmed

1 red bell pepper, cut into 16 pieces

Peanut Sauce

1 can (about 13 ounces) unsweetened coconut milk

½ cup creamy peanut butter

2 tablespoons packed brown sugar

1 tablespoon rice vinegar

2 teaspoons red Thai curry paste

Place tofu on cutting board on several layers of paper towels. Cover with additional paper towels and weigh down with another cutting board, heavy plate or saucepan. Let stand 15 to 20 minutes.

1. Cut tofu into 24 cubes. Combine water, soy sauce, sesame oil, garlic and ginger in small bowl. Place tofu, mushrooms and bell pepper in large resealable food storage bag. Add soy sauce mixture; seal bag and turn gently to coat. Marinate 30 minutes, turning occasionally. Soak eight 8-inch bamboo skewers in water 20 minutes.

2. Preheat oven to 400°F. Spray baking sheet with nonstick cooking spray.

3. Drain tofu mixture; discard marinade. Thread tofu, mushrooms and bell pepper onto skewers. Place skewers on prepared baking sheet.

4. Bake 25 minutes or until tofu cubes are lightly browned and vegetables are softened.

5. Meanwhile, whisk coconut milk, peanut butter, brown sugar, vinegar and curry paste in small saucepan over medium heat. Bring to a boil, stirring constantly. Immediately reduce heat to low; cook about 20 minutes or until creamy and thick, stirring frequently. Serve satay with sauce.

—— **Makes 4 servings**

Roasted Butternut Squash Bowl

1 butternut squash (about 2½ pounds)

¼ cup olive oil, divided

1 teaspoon salt

1 teaspoon dried thyme

½ teaspoon black pepper

¼ cup orange juice

2 tablespoons maple syrup

2 tablespoons cider vinegar

2 cloves garlic, minced

1 teaspoon grated orange peel

⅛ teaspoon red pepper flakes (optional)

1 cup uncooked wild rice blend or basmati rice

2 cups shredded red cabbage, Napa cabbage or lettuce

1 cucumber, thinly sliced

2 teaspoons toasted white sesame seeds* or black sesame seeds

To toast sesame seeds, spread in small skillet. Shake skillet over medium-low heat 2 minutes or until seeds begin to pop and turn golden brown.

1. Preheat oven to 425°F. Peel squash and cut in half lengthwise. Scoop out seeds with a spoon; discard or set aside to roast (see Note). Cut squash crosswise into ¼-inch slices.

2. Combine squash, 2 tablespoons oil, salt, thyme and black pepper in large bowl; stir until squash is evenly coated with oil and seasonings. Spread squash in single layer on two large baking sheets. Bake 30 minutes or until squash is tender and browned, turning once or twice.

3. For glaze, whisk orange juice, maple syrup, vinegar, garlic, orange peel, remaining 2 tablespoons oil and red pepper flakes, if desired, in small saucepan until well blended. Cook over medium-low heat 10 minutes or until glaze is syrupy and reduced by half, stirring frequently. Brush half of mixture over squash; bake 5 minutes or until squash is glazed.

4. Meanwhile, cook rice according to package directions. Divide rice, cabbage and cucumber among four serving bowls; top with squash. Drizzle with remaining glaze and sprinkle with sesame seeds.

—— Makes 4 servings

Note: To roast the squash seeds, separate the seeds from the stringy parts of the squash; place in small bowl. Add 1 teaspoon olive oil and season with salt and black pepper. Line a small baking sheet with foil; spread seeds on foil. Bake at 350°F for 12 to 15 minutes or until seeds are browned and crisp, stirring occasionally.

SANDWICHES

BBQ Portobello Sandwiches

1 teaspoon salt

1 teaspoon smoked paprika

1 teaspoon onion powder

½ teaspoon garlic powder

½ teaspoon ground cumin

½ teaspoon black pepper

4 portobello mushroom caps

2 tablespoons plus 1 teaspoon olive oil, divided

½ medium yellow onion, finely chopped

¼ cup ketchup

2 tablespoons apple cider vinegar

1 tablespoon Dijon mustard

1 tablespoon packed brown sugar

1 teaspoon soy sauce

4 hamburger buns

Sliced dill pickles and/or shredded cabbage

1. Preheat oven to 375°F. Line baking sheet with parchment paper.

2. Combine salt, paprika, onion powder, garlic powder, cumin and pepper in small bowl. Scrape gills from mushrooms and remove any stem. Cut mushrooms into ½-inch slices; place in large bowl. Drizzle with 2 tablespoons oil; toss to coat. Add seasoning mixture; toss until well blended. Arrange slices in single layer on prepared baking sheet.

3. Bake 15 minutes. Turn and bake 5 minutes or until mushrooms are tender and have shrunken slightly.

4. Meanwhile, heat remaining 1 teaspoon oil in small saucepan over medium-high heat. Add onion; cook and stir 5 minutes or until onion is very soft. Add ketchup, vinegar, mustard, brown sugar and soy sauce; mix well. Reduce heat to low; simmer 5 minutes. Combine mushrooms and sauce in large bowl; mix well. Serve on buns with desired toppings.

—— **Makes 4 servings**

Peanut Carrot Roll-Ups

½ cup peanut butter

2 (6- to 7-inch) whole wheat or spinach tortillas

½ cup finely chopped apple

¼ cup shredded carrot

2 tablespoons honey

1. Spread peanut butter evenly over one side of each tortilla.

2. Combine apple and carrot in small bowl. Sprinkle mixture over peanut butter, covering most of tortilla and leaving one side uncovered.

3. Drizzle honey evenly over apple mixture. Starting from edge nearest filling, roll up tortillas. Cut tortillas in half crosswise. Serve immediately or wrap in plastic wrap and refrigerate until ready to serve.

—— Makes 2 to 4 servings

Farro Veggie Burgers

1½ cups water

½ cup uncooked pearled farro

2 medium potatoes, peeled and quartered

2 to 4 tablespoons canola oil, divided

¾ cup finely chopped green onions

1 cup grated carrots

2 teaspoons grated fresh ginger

2 tablespoons ground almonds

¼ to ¾ teaspoon salt

¼ teaspoon black pepper

½ cup panko bread crumbs

6 whole wheat hamburger buns

Lettuce leaves

Ketchup and mustard (optional)

1. Combine 1½ cups water and farro in medium saucepan; bring to a boil over high heat. Reduce heat to low; partially cover and cook 25 to 30 minutes or until farro is tender. Drain and cool.

2. Meanwhile, place potatoes in large saucepan; cover with water. Bring to a boil; reduce heat and simmer 20 minutes or until tender. Cool and mash potatoes; set aside.

3. Heat 1 tablespoon oil in medium skillet over medium-high heat. Add green onions; cook and stir 1 minute. Add carrots and ginger; cover and cook 2 to 3 minutes or until carrots are tender. Transfer to large bowl; cool completely.

4. Add mashed potatoes and farro to carrot mixture. Add almonds, salt and pepper; mix well. Shape mixture into six patties. Spread panko on medium plate; coat patties with panko.

5. Heat 1 tablespoon oil in large nonstick skillet over medium heat. Cook patties about 4 minutes per side or until golden brown, adding additional oil as needed. Serve on buns with lettuce and desired condiments.

—— **Makes 6 servings**

Mediterranean Vegetable Sandwiches

1 small eggplant, peeled, halved and cut into ¼-inch-thick slices

Salt

1 small zucchini, halved and cut lengthwise into ¼-inch-thick slices

1 red bell pepper, sliced

3 tablespoons balsamic vinegar

½ teaspoon garlic powder

2 French bread rolls, cut in half lengthwise

Hummus, tahini sauce or tzatziki sauce (optional)

1. Place eggplant in colander; lightly sprinkle with salt. Let stand 30 minutes. Rinse eggplant; pat dry with paper towels.

2. Preheat broiler. Spray rack with nonstick cooking spray. Place vegetables on rack. Broil 4 inches from heat source 8 to 10 minutes or until vegetables are browned, turning once.

3. Whisk vinegar and garlic powder in medium bowl until well blended. Add vegetables; toss to coat evenly. Serve vegetables on rolls with desired sauce.

—— **Makes 2 servings**

Note: If you don't have a broiler rack, line a baking sheet with foil and place a wire cooling rack on top. Spray the rack with nonstick cooking spray.

"Bacon" and Avocado Sandwiches

12 slices vegetarian bacon

½ ripe avocado

2 tablespoons sour cream or mayonnaise (vegan or regular)

1 teaspoon fresh lemon juice

8 thin slices whole wheat sandwich bread, toasted

8 thin tomato slices

1 cup alfalfa sprouts

1. Cook bacon according to package directions.

2. Combine avocado, yogurt and lemon juice in small bowl; stir with fork until smooth. Spread about 1 tablespoon avocado mixture on 1 side of 4 bread slices.

3. Top each with 3 slices bacon, 2 slices tomato, ¼ cup alfalfa sprouts and remaining bread slice.

—— **Makes 4 servings**

Mushroom Tofu Burgers

7 ounces extra firm tofu

3 tablespoons boiling water

1 tablespoon ground flaxseed

3 teaspoons olive oil, divided

1 package (8 ounces) cremini mushrooms, coarsely chopped

½ medium onion, coarsely chopped

1 clove garlic, minced

1 cup old-fashioned oats

⅓ cup finely chopped walnuts

½ teaspoon salt

½ teaspoon onion powder

¼ teaspoon dried thyme

6 multigrain English muffins or sandwich rolls, split and toasted

Lettuce, tomato and red onion slices (optional)

1. Crumble tofu and spread on small baking sheet or freezer-safe plate. Freeze 1 hour or until firm. Combine boiling water and flaxseed in small bowl; let stand until completely cool.

2. Heat 1 teaspoon oil in large nonstick skillet over medium heat. Add mushrooms, onion and garlic; cook and stir 10 minutes or until mushrooms have released most of their juices. Remove from heat; cool slightly.

3. Combine mushroom mixture, tofu, oats, walnuts, flaxseed mixture, salt, onion powder and thyme in food processor or blender; process until combined. (Some tofu pieces may remain). Shape mixture into six ⅓-cup patties.

4. Heat 1 teaspoon oil in same skillet over medium-low heat. Working in batches, cook patties 5 minutes per side. Repeat with remaining oil and patties. Serve on English muffins with lettuce, tomato and red onion, if desired.

—— **Makes 6 servings**

Tofu, Black Bean and Corn Chili Burritos

1 can (about 15 ounces) black beans, rinsed and drained

1 can (about 14 ounces) diced tomatoes with green pepper, celery and onion

8 ounces firm tofu, crumbled

1 cup salsa

1 cup vegetable broth

½ cup frozen corn

1 tablespoon chili powder

1 teaspoon ground cumin

1 teaspoon salt

½ teaspoon ground chipotle pepper

½ teaspoon dried oregano

1 cup uncooked rice

Flour tortillas (8 to 10 inches)

Optional toppings: sliced avocado, lettuce and/or chopped fresh cilantro

1. Combine beans, tomatoes, tofu, salsa, broth, corn, chili powder, cumin, salt, chipotle pepper and oregano in large saucepan. Cover and cook over medium-low heat 45 minutes to 1 hour or until flavors have blended, stirring occasionally and adding water by tablespoons if mixture seems dry.

2. Meanwhile, cook rice according to package directions. Stir rice into bean mixture.

3. Top each tortilla with about 1½ cups bean mixture. Fold short ends of each tortilla over part of filling then roll up jelly-roll style. Serve with desired toppings.

—— Makes 8 servings

Roasted Eggplant Panini

3 tablespoons olive oil, divided

1 medium eggplant (about 1¼ pounds)

1 cup mozzarella-style vegan cheese alternative shreds

1 tablespoon chopped fresh basil

1 tablespoon fresh lemon juice

⅛ teaspoon salt

8 slices (1 ounce each) whole grain Italian bread

1. Preheat oven to 400°F. Line baking sheet with parchment paper; brush with 1 tablespoon oil. Slice eggplant in half lengthwise. Place cut sides down on prepared baking sheet. Roast 45 minutes. Let stand 15 minutes or until cool enough to handle.

2. Meanwhile, combine cheese alternative, basil, lemon juice and salt in small bowl; set aside.

3. Cut each eggplant piece in half. Remove pulp; discard skin. Place one fourth of eggplant on each of 4 bread slices, pressing gently into bread. Top evenly with cheese alternative mixture. Top with remaining bread slices. Brush outsides of sandwiches with remaining 2 tablespoons olive oil.

4. Heat large nonstick grill pan or skillet over medium heat. Cook sandwiches 3 to 4 minutes per side, pressing down with spatula until cheese alternative is melted and bread is toasted. (Cover pan during last minute of cooking to melt cheese, if desired.) Serve immediately.

—— **Makes 4 sandwiches**

Caprese Portobello Burgers

1 cup mozzarella-
    style vegan cheese
    alternative shreds

2 plum tomatoes, chopped

2 tablespoons chopped
    fresh basil

1 tablespoon balsamic
    vinaigrette

1 clove garlic, crushed

¼ teaspoon salt

⅛ teaspoon black pepper

4 portobello mushrooms
    (about ¾ pound), gills
    and stems removed

4 whole wheat sandwich
    thin rounds, toasted

1. Spray grid with nonstick cooking spray. Prepare grill for direct cooking over medium-high heat. Meanwhile, combine cheese alternative, tomatoes, basil, vinaigrette, garlic, salt and pepper in small bowl.

2. Grill mushroom caps, stem side down, 5 minutes per side or until browned and tender. Spoon one fourth of tomato mixture into each cap. Cover and grill 3 minutes or until cheese alternative is melted. Serve stuffed mushrooms on sandwich thins.

—— **Makes 4 servings**

Note: Mushrooms can be broiled instead of grilled. Preheat broiler. Line baking sheet with foil; spray with nonstick cooking spray. Place mushrooms, cap side up, on baking sheet. Broil 5 minutes per side. Fill caps with tomato mixture and broil 3 minutes.

SNACKS & BREADS

Buffalo Cauliflower Bites

¾ cup all-purpose flour

¼ cup cornstarch

1 teaspoon salt

½ teaspoon garlic powder

¼ teaspoon black pepper

1 cup water

1 large head cauliflower (2½ pounds), cut into 1-inch florets

½ cup hot pepper sauce

¼ cup (½ stick) regular or vegan plant butter, melted

Blue cheese or ranch dressing and celery sticks for serving

1. Preheat oven to 450°F. Line baking sheet with foil; spray with nonstick cooking spray.

2. Whisk flour, cornstarch, salt, garlic powder and black pepper in large bowl. Whisk in water until smooth and well blended. Add cauliflower to batter in batches; stir to coat. Remove with slotted spoon, letting excess batter drip back into bowl. Arrange on prepared baking sheet.

3. Bake 20 minutes or until cauliflower is lightly browned. Combine hot pepper sauce and butter in small bowl; mix well. Pour over cauliflower; toss until well blended. Bake 5 to 10 minutes or until cauliflower is glazed and crisp, stirring once. Serve with blue cheese or ranch dressing and celery sticks.

—— Makes 8 servings

Snack Attack Mix

- 4 cups unsweetened corn cereal squares or whole wheat cereal squares
- 1 cup pretzels sticks, broken in half
- 1 cup multigrain pita chips, broken into bite-size pieces
- 1 cup slivered almonds
- 2 tablespoons vegan Worcestershire sauce or soy sauce
- 2 teaspoons canola oil
- 2 teaspoons paprika
- 1½ teaspoons cider vinegar
- 1 teaspoon dry mustard
- 1 teaspoon garlic powder
- 1 teaspoon salt
- ½ teaspoon ground cumin
- ¼ teaspoon ground red pepper

1. Preheat oven to 300°F. Combine cereal, pretzels, pita chips and almonds in large bowl.

2. Combine Worcestershire sauce, oil, paprika, vinegar, mustard, garlic powder, salt, cumin and red pepper in small bowl; stir until well blended. Spoon over cereal mixture; toss gently until well coated. Spread evenly on large baking sheet.

3. Bake 10 to 15 minutes or until lightly browned, stirring every 5 minutes. Cool on baking sheet on wire rack 2 hours. Store in airtight container.

—— Makes 7 cups

Note: For a sweet and salty snack mix, stir ½ teaspoon dried cranberries, cherries or raisins into cooled snack mix.

Crunchy Whole Grain Bread

2 cups warm water (105° to 115°F), divided

⅓ cup honey

2 tablespoons vegetable oil

1 tablespoon salt

2 packages (¼ ounce each) active dry yeast

2 to 2½ cups whole wheat flour, divided

1 cup bread flour

1¼ cups quick oats, divided

½ cup raw or roasted pepitas or sunflower kernels

½ cup assorted grains and seeds (such as quinoa, millet, chia seeds or flax seeds)

1. Combine 1½ cups warm water, honey, oil and salt in small saucepan; heat over low heat until warm (115° to 120°F), stirring occasionally.

2. Dissolve yeast in remaining ½ cup warm water in large bowl of stand mixer; let stand 5 minutes. Stir in honey mixture. Add 1 cup whole wheat flour and bread flour; mix with dough hook at low speed 2 minutes. Slowly add 1 cup oats, pepitas and assorted grains; mix until incorporated. Add remaining whole wheat flour, ½ cup at a time; knead until dough begins to form a ball. Knead 6 to 8 minutes or until dough is smooth and elastic.

3. Place dough in large lightly greased bowl; turn to grease top. Cover and let rise in warm place 1½ to 2 hours or until doubled in size.

4. Spray two 9×5-inch loaf pans with nonstick cooking spray. Punch down dough. Divide dough in half; shape each half into a loaf. Place in prepared pans. Cover and let rise in warm place 1 hour or until almost doubled in size.

5. Preheat oven to 375°F. Sprinkle remaining ¼ cup oats over tops of loaves.

6. Bake 35 to 45 minutes or until breads sound hollow when tapped. Cool in pans 10 minutes. Remove to wire racks; cool completely.

—— **Makes 2 loaves**

Two Tomato Kalamata Crostini

1 medium baguette, cut into 20 (¼-inch-thick) slices

8 sun-dried tomatoes (not packed in oil)

1 cup grape tomatoes, chopped

12 kalamata olives, pitted and finely chopped

2 teaspoons cider vinegar

1½ teaspoons dried basil

1 teaspoon olive oil

⅛ teaspoon salt

1 clove garlic, halved crosswise

1. Preheat oven to 350°F. Place bread slices on large baking sheet. Bake 10 minutes or until edges are golden brown. Cool on wire rack.

2. Place sun-dried tomatoes in medium bowl; cover with boiling water. Let stand 10 minutes. Drain and chop tomatoes.

3. Combine sun-dried tomatoes, grape tomatoes, olives, vinegar, basil, oil and salt in medium bowl; mix well.

4. Rub bread slices with garlic. Top each bread slice with tomato mixture.

—— **Makes 20 servings**

Hummus-Filled Veggie Bites

½ **clove garlic**

1 **can (about 15 ounces) chickpeas, rinsed and drained**

¼ **cup tahini**

2 **tablespoons lemon juice**

½ **teaspoon salt**

¼ **teaspoon ground cumin**

2 **to 4 tablespoons ice water**

16 **white mushrooms**

¼ **cup thinly sliced roasted red pepper**

16 **grape or cherry tomatoes**

16 **snow peas, trimmed, or cucumber slices**

1. With motor running, drop garlic through feed tube of food processor. Add chickpeas; process until pasty. Add tahini, lemon juice, salt and cumin; process until combined. With motor running, add ice water through feed tube by tablespoonfuls until mixture is smooth. Process 2 minutes or until very smooth and fluffy, scraping down side of bowl as needed.

2. Wipe mushrooms clean with damp paper towel and remove stems. Scoop out caps slightly with small melon ball scoop or spoon. Using teaspoon, fill each mushroom cap with hummus, mounding slightly. Place mushrooms on serving plate. Top with red pepper strips.

3. Halve tomatoes lengthwise. Using small spoon, scrape out seeds, juice and membranes. Place tomato halves cut sides down on paper towels to drain. Using teaspoon, fill tomato halves with hummus, mounding slightly. Place on serving plate with mushrooms.

4. Spread remaining hummus on curved sides of snow peas. Place on serving plate. Serve immediately or cover loosely with plastic wrap and refrigerate until ready to serve.

—— **Makes 48 appetizers**

Sweet Onion and Pepita Flatbread

1 package (¼ ounce) active dry yeast

½ teaspoon sugar

⅔ cup warm water (105° to 115°F)

2 to 2¼ cups all-purpose flour

2 tablespoons olive oil

¾ teaspoon salt, divided

¼ cup canola oil

2 red onions, thinly sliced

¼ cup raw pepitas

½ teaspoon dried oregano

⅛ teaspoon red pepper flakes

⅛ teaspoon black pepper

1. Dissolve yeast and sugar in warm water in large bowl of stand mixer fitted with dough hook; let stand 5 minutes or until bubbly.

2. Add 2 cups flour, olive oil and ½ teaspoon salt; knead on low speed 5 to 7 minutes or until dough is smooth and elastic, adding additional flour, 1 tablespoon at a time, if necessary to clean side of bowl. Shape dough into a ball. Place in large lightly greased bowl; turn to grease top. Cover and let rise in warm place about 1 hour or until doubled in size.

3. Preheat oven to 400°F. Line baking sheet with parchment paper or spray with nonstick cooking spray. Roll out dough into 15×10-inch rectangle; place on prepared baking sheet. Bake 10 minutes.

4. Meanwhile, heat canola oil in large skillet over medium-high heat. Add onions; cook and stir 7 minutes or until tender. Add pepitas, oregano, remaining ¼ teaspoon salt, red pepper flakes and black pepper; cook and stir 3 minutes. Spread onion mixture evenly over partially baked crust.

5. Bake 10 to 14 minutes or until crust is golden and onions begin to brown. Let stand 5 minutes before cutting.

—— Makes 10 servings

Cauliflower Socca

2 cups chickpea flour

1¾ teaspoons salt

¼ teaspoon black pepper

2 cups water

½ cup olive oil, divided

1½ cups finely chopped
    cauliflower

1 can (about 15 ounces)
    chickpeas, rinsed and
    drained

2 tablespoons chopped
    fresh cilantro or parsley

1. Whisk chickpea flour, salt and pepper in large bowl to remove any lumps. Whisk in water and ¼ cup oil. Let stand at room temperature 30 minutes.

2. Meanwhile, preheat oven to 450°F. Place 12-inch cast iron skillet in oven to preheat at least 10 minutes. Pour remaining ¼ cup oil into hot skillet. Add cauliflower and chickpeas. Bake 10 minutes.

3. Whisk cilantro into batter; pour batter over cauliflower and chickpeas in skillet. Bake 15 minutes or until edge is lightly browned, top is firm and toothpick inserted into center comes out with moist crumbs. Cut into wedges; serve warm or at room temperature.

—— **Makes 8 servings**

Mediterranean Flatbread

1 package (¼ ounce) active dry yeast

½ teaspoon sugar

⅔ cup warm water (105° to 115°F)

2 to 2¼ cups all-purpose flour

4 tablespoons olive oil, divided

¾ teaspoon salt, divided

1 cup thinly sliced onion

½ cup thinly sliced red bell pepper

½ cup thinly sliced green bell pepper

2 cloves garlic, minced

½ teaspoon dried rosemary

⅛ teaspoon red pepper flakes (optional)

½ cup pitted kalamata olives, coarsely chopped

1. Dissolve yeast and sugar in warm water in large bowl of stand mixer fitted with dough hook; let stand 5 minutes or until bubbly.

2. Add 2 cups flour, 2 tablespoons oil and ½ teaspoon salt; mix at low speed 5 to 7 minutes or dough is smooth and elastic, adding additional flour, 1 tablespoon at a time, if necessary to clean side of bowl.

3. Shape dough into a ball. Place dough in large lightly greased bowl; turn to grease top. Cover and let rise in warm place about 1 hour or until doubled in size.

4. Preheat oven to 350°F.

5. Heat 1 tablespoon oil in large skillet over medium-high heat. Add onion and bell peppers; cook and stir 5 minutes or until onion begins to brown. Remove from heat. Season with remaining ¼ teaspoon salt.

6. Roll out dough into 17×12-inch rectangle; place on baking sheet. Combine garlic and remaining 1 tablespoon oil in small bowl; spread evenly over dough. Sprinkle with rosemary and red pepper flakes, if desired. Top with onion mixture; sprinkle with olives.

7. Bake 16 to 18 minutes or until golden brown. Cut flatbread in half lengthwise; cut crosswise into 1-inch-wide strips.

—— **Makes about 32 pieces**

Vietnamese Vegetable Spring Rolls

Dipping Sauce

- 2 tablespoons creamy peanut butter
- 2 tablespoons water
- 1 tablespoon soy sauce
- ⅓ cup hoisin sauce
- ½ teaspoon toasted sesame oil
- 1 clove garlic, minced
- Dash hot pepper sauce

Spring Rolls

- 12 dried mushrooms (1 ounce)
- 1 large carrot, julienned
- 2 teaspoons sugar, divided
- 3 cups plus 2 tablespoons vegetable oil, divided
- 1 medium yellow onion, sliced
- 1 clove garlic, minced
- 1 tablespoon soy sauce
- 1 teaspoon toasted sesame oil
- 1½ cups fresh bean sprouts (4 ounces), rinsed and drained
- 14 (7-inch) egg roll wrappers
- 1 egg, beaten

1. For dipping sauce, whisk peanut butter, 2 tablespoons water and 1 tablespoon soy sauce in small bowl until smooth. Add hoisin sauce, ½ teaspoon sesame oil, 1 clove garlic and hot pepper sauce; mix until well blended. Refrigerate until ready to serve.

2. Place mushrooms in bowl; cover with hot water. Let stand 30 minutes. Drain mushrooms, reserving ½ cup liquid. Squeeze out excess water. Cut stems off mushrooms; discard. Cut caps into thin slices; set aside.

3. Meanwhile, combine carrot and 1 teaspoon sugar in medium bowl. Let stand 15 minutes, tossing occasionally.

4. Heat wok over medium-high heat 1 minute or until hot. Drizzle 2 tablespoons vegetable oil into wok and heat 30 seconds. Add onion; stir-fry 1 minute. Stir in mushrooms, 1 clove garlic and reserved mushroom liquid. Reduce heat to medium. Cover and cook 3 minutes or until mushrooms are tender. Add 1 tablespoon soy sauce, 1 teaspoon sesame oil and remaining 1 teaspoon sugar; cook and stir 3 to 5 minutes or until all liquid has evaporated. Transfer mushroom mixture to medium bowl; set aside to cool slightly.

5. Add carrot strips and bean sprouts to mushroom mixture; toss lightly. Place 1 wrapper on work surface with one corner facing you, keeping remaining wrappers covered with plastic wrap. Drain mushroom mixture; place 3 tablespoons mixture on bottom third of wrapper. Brush edges of wrapper with some beaten egg.

6. To form spring rolls, fold bottom corner of wrapper up over filling. Fold in and overlap the opposite right and left corners to form 3½-inch-wide log. Roll up filling to remaining corner and place spring roll on tray covered with plastic wrap. Repeat with remaining wrappers and filling.

7. Heat remaining 3 cups vegetable oil in wok over high heat to 375°F; adjust heat to maintain temperature during cooking. Working in batches of 3 to 4, fry rolls 2 to 3 minutes or until golden brown, turning once. Drain on paper towels. Serve with sauce.

—— Makes 14 rolls

No-Knead Sandwich Bread

¾ **cup warm water (110° to 115°F)**

2 **packages (¼ ounce each; 4½ teaspoons) active dry yeast**

3 **tablespoons canola oil**

1 **cup all-purpose flour**

⅔ **cup old-fashioned oats**

¼ **cup soy flour**

¼ **cup vital wheat gluten**

¼ **cup sesame seeds**

2 **teaspoons sugar**

1 **teaspoon salt**

1. Combine warm water and yeast in small bowl; stir to dissolve yeast. Let stand 5 minutes. Stir in oil.

2. Combine all-purpose flour, oats, soy flour, vital wheat gluten, sesame seeds, sugar and salt in food processor fitted with plastic dough blade. Using on/off pulses, process until well blended.

3. With motor running, slowly pour yeast mixture through feed tube; pulse until dough forms ball. Unlock processor lid, but do not remove; let dough rise 1 hour or until doubled in size.

4. Spray 8×4-inch loaf pan with nonstick cooking spray. Pulse briefly until dough forms ball. Turn out dough onto lightly floured work surface. Shape into a disc. (Dough will be slightly sticky.) Roll dough into 12×8-inch rectangle. Roll up from short side; fold under ends and place in prepared pan. Cover and let rise in warm place 45 minutes or until doubled in size.

5. Preheat oven to 375°F. Bake 35 minutes or until bread is golden brown and sounds hollow when tapped. Remove from pan; cool completely on wire rack.

—— Makes 1 loaf

Guacamole Bites

2 tablespoons vegetable oil

1¼ teaspoons salt, divided

½ teaspoon garlic powder

12 (6-inch) corn tortillas

2 small ripe avocados

2 tablespoons finely chopped onion

1 tablespoon chopped fresh cilantro

2 teaspoons lime juice

1 teaspoon finely chopped jalapeño pepper *or* ¼ teaspoon hot pepper sauce

1. Preheat oven to 375°F. Whisk oil, ¾ teaspoon salt and garlic powder in small bowl until well blended.

2. Use 3-inch biscuit cutter to cut out two circles from each tortilla to create 24 circles total. Wrap stack of tortilla circles loosely in waxed paper; microwave on HIGH 10 to 15 seconds or just until softened. Brush one side of each tortilla very lightly with oil mixture; press into 24 mini (1¾-inch) muffin cups, oiled side up. (Do not spray muffin cups with nonstick cooking spray.)

3. Bake about 8 minutes or until crisp. Remove to wire racks to cool.

4. Meanwhile, prepare guacamole. Cut avocados into halves; remove pits. Scoop pulp into large bowl; coarsely mash, leaving avocado slightly chunky. Stir in onion, cilantro, lime juice, remaining ½ teaspoon salt and jalapeño; mix well.

5. Fill each tortilla cup with 2 to 3 teaspoons guacamole.

—— **Makes 24 bites**

MORNING MEALS

Fruited Granola

3 cups quick-cooking oats

1 cup sliced almonds

1 cup honey

½ cup wheat germ

3 tablespoons butter or vegan plant butter, melted

1 teaspoon ground cinnamon

3 cups whole grain cereal flakes

½ cup dried blueberries or golden raisins

½ cup dried cranberries or cherries

½ cup dried banana chips or chopped pitted dates

1. Preheat oven to 325°F.

2. Spread oats and almonds in single layer in 13×9-inch baking pan. Bake 15 minutes or until lightly toasted, stirring frequently.

3. Combine honey, wheat germ, butter and cinnamon in large bowl until well blended. Add oats and almonds; toss to coat completely. Spread mixture in single layer in baking pan. Bake 20 minutes or until golden brown. Cool completely in pan on wire rack. Break mixture into chunks.

4. Combine oat chunks, cereal, blueberries, cranberries and banana chips in large bowl. Store in airtight container at room temperature up to 2 weeks.

—— **Makes about 20 servings**

No-Bake Fruit and Grain Bars

½ **cup cooked amaranth***

2 **cups whole grain puffed rice cereal**

½ **cup chopped dried fruit**

½ **cup honey or maple syrup**

¼ **cup sugar**

¾ **cup almond butter**

> *Amaranth can be found in health food stores in the bulk bins. It may also be found in large supermarkets in the health food aisle.*

1. Spray 8- or 9-inch square baking pan with nonstick cooking spray.

2. Heat medium saucepan over high heat. Add 1 tablespoon amaranth; stir or gently shake saucepan until almost all seeds have popped. (Partially cover saucepan if seeds are popping over the side.) Remove to medium bowl. Repeat with remaining amaranth.

3. Stir cereal and dried fruit into popped amaranth.

4. Combine honey and sugar in same saucepan; bring to a boil over medium heat. Remove from heat; stir in almond butter until melted and smooth.

5. Pour honey mixture over cereal mixture; stir until evenly coated. Press firmly into prepared pan. Let stand until set. Cut into bars.

—— **Makes 16 bars**

Strawberry and Peach Crisp

1 cup frozen unsweetened peach slices, thawed and cut into 1-inch pieces

1 cup sliced fresh strawberries

3 teaspoons sugar, divided

¼ cup bran cereal flakes

2 tablespoons old-fashioned oats

1 tablespoon all-purpose flour

⅛ teaspoon ground cinnamon

⅛ teaspoon salt

1 tablespoon butter or vegan plant butter, cut into small pieces

Plain yogurt or Greek yogurt (optional)

1. Preheat oven to 325°F. Spray 1- to 1½-quart baking dish with nonstick cooking spray.

2. Combine peaches and strawberries in prepared baking dish. Sprinkle with 1 teaspoon sugar.

3. Combine cereal, oats, flour, cinnamon and salt in bowl. Stir in remaining 2 teaspoons sugar. Add butter; mix with fingertips until mixture resembles coarse crumbs. Sprinkle over fruit in baking dish.

4. Bake 20 minutes or until filling is bubbly and topping is lightly browned. Serve warm with yogurt, if desired.

—— **Makes 2 to 4 servings**

Overnight Chia Oat Pudding

1 cup old-fashioned oats

¼ cup chia seeds

3 tablespoons palm sugar or packed brown sugar, divided

½ teaspoon ground cinnamon

½ teaspoon salt

1¾ cups oatmilk

1 package (1 pound) fresh strawberries, stemmed and diced

1 cup fresh blueberries (optional)

4 tablespoons chopped pecans or sliced almonds

4 bananas, sliced (optional)

1. Combine oats, chia seeds, 2 tablespoons sugar, cinnamon and salt in medium bowl or food storage container. Add oatmilk; stir until well blended. Cover and refrigerate overnight.

2. Combine strawberries and remaining 1 tablespoon sugar in another medium bowl or food storage container. Cover and refrigerate overnight.

3. Stir oat mixture. For each serving, scoop ½ cup oat mixture into bowl. Top with strawberries, blueberries, if desired, and pecans. Serve with bananas, if desired.

—— **Makes 4 servings**

Peanut Butter Berry Bars

2 cups instant oatmeal

⅓ cup plus 2 tablespoons semisweet mini chocolate chips, divided

½ cup peanut butter

¼ cup packed brown sugar

3 tablespoons canola oil

2 tablespoons all-purpose flour

1 teaspoon ground cinnamon

¾ cup finely chopped strawberries

1. Preheat oven to 350°F. Heat large skillet over medium-high heat. Add oatmeal; cook and stir 4 to 5 minutes or until lightly browned. Immediately remove from skillet to medium bowl.

2. Place ⅓ cup chips in medium microwavable bowl. Microwave 1 minute on HIGH. Stir chips; microwave at additional 15-second intervals until chips are melted. Stir in peanut butter, brown sugar, oil, flour and cinnamon until well blended. Stir in oatmeal.

3. Press oatmeal mixture onto bottom of 9-inch square baking pan. Bake 10 to 12 minutes or until top is lightly browned. Cool completely in pan on wire rack.

4. Top crust with strawberries. Place remaining 2 tablespoons chips in small resealable food storage bag. Seal. Microwave 30 seconds on HIGH. Cut off tiny corner of bag; drizzle chocolate over strawberries. Cover and freeze at least 2 hours or until ready to serve.

5. To serve, let stand at room temperature 10 minutes. Cut into bars. Store leftovers in freezer.

—— **Makes 16 bars**

Metric Conversion Chart

VOLUME MEASUREMENTS (dry)

⅛ teaspoon = 0.5 mL
¼ teaspoon = 1 mL
½ teaspoon = 2 mL
¾ teaspoon = 4 mL
1 teaspoon = 5 mL
1 tablespoon = 15 mL
2 tablespoons = 30 mL
¼ cup = 60 mL
⅓ cup = 75 mL
½ cup = 125 mL
⅔ cup = 150 mL
¾ cup = 175 mL
1 cup = 250 mL
2 cups = 1 pint = 500 mL
3 cups = 750 mL
4 cups = 1 quart = 1 L

VOLUME MEASUREMENTS (fluid)

1 fluid ounce (2 tablespoons) = 30 mL
4 fluid ounces (½ cup) = 125 mL
8 fluid ounces (1 cup) = 250 mL
12 fluid ounces (1½ cups) = 375 mL
16 fluid ounces (2 cups) = 500 mL

WEIGHTS (mass)

½ ounce = 15 g
1 ounce = 30 g
3 ounces = 90 g
4 ounces = 120 g
8 ounces = 225 g
10 ounces = 285 g
12 ounces = 360 g
16 ounces = 1 pound = 450 g

DIMENSIONS

1/16 inch = 2 mm
⅛ inch = 3 mm
¼ inch = 6 mm
½ inch = 1.5 cm
¾ inch = 2 cm
1 inch = 2.5 cm

OVEN TEMPERATURES

250°F = 120°C
275°F = 140°C
300°F = 150°C
325°F = 160°C
350°F = 180°C
375°F = 190°C
400°F = 200°C
425°F = 220°C
450°F = 230°C

BAKING PAN SIZES

Utensil	Size in Inches/Quarts	Metric Volume	Size in Centimeters
Baking or Cake Pan (square or rectangular)	8×8×2	2 L	20×20×5
	9×9×2	2.5 L	23×23×5
	12×8×2	3 L	30×20×5
	13×9×2	3.5 L	33×23×5
Loaf Pan	8×4×3	1.5 L	20×10×7
	9×5×3	2 L	23×13×7
Round Layer Cake Pan	8×1½	1.2 L	20×4
	9×1½	1.5 L	23×4
Pie Plate	8×1¼	750 mL	20×3
	9×1¼	1 L	23×3
Baking Dish or Casserole	1 quart	1 L	—
	1½ quart	1.5 L	—
	2 quart	2 L	—